Thomas Krieger

kids
IN THE
GARDEN

THE AUSTRALIAN
Women's Weekly

kids
IN THE
GARDEN

gardening·craft·cooking

Mary Moody

acp
books

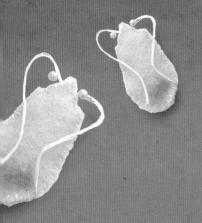

foreword

Every child is born a naturalist. Once upon a summer time, babies slept outdoors in the afternoons, under a tree in their prams covered with a mosquito net. The leaves rustling and the busy birds twittering through the branches were their lullaby, and fresh air filled their lungs as they blissfully dreamed away. When they could sit upright, unassisted, it was often on a blanket in a shady corner of the lawn. They pushed the blanket aside and ran their small chubby fingers through the grass in sensory delight.

As toddlers it was water play in a bucket, then mud pies and eventually they climbed the trees under which they had once slept so peacefully. They brought inside all manner of creatures for their parents to inspect, from earwigs to slaters, from snails to frogs and spiders. They studied bird's nests and collected cicada shells and they experienced the fascinating world in their own backyards.

Today's kids have more protected and structured indoor lives and yet, with just a little prodding from us, they can take to the outdoors again and reap the joys of engaging with the natural world. They have an amazing capacity to observe and learn, and their curiosity and enthusiasm will develop into a love of gardens and the mysteries of the wider world. It will stay with them for the rest of their lives. You may need to do some of the initial spadework, setting up an outdoor environment that can foster this passion. Initially you may need to work with them, guiding and encouraging. Then in time they will become more independent and adventurous, and you will find them heading out to the garden to check if any of their tomatoes have ripened, or if there is corn ready for picking.

Introducing children to the pleasures of nature through gardening is one of the most positive contributions a parent can make. I have nurtured this joy in my own children and now I have the infinite pleasure of introducing my nine grandchildren to the delights of the garden.

Mary Moody

Here I am with three of my grandchildren – Ella, Caius and Gus at the front who looks keen to get into a bit of hedge pruning. They love to help in the garden, especially if there is corn to be picked or potatoes to be dug up at the end of summer.

Contents

what to wear

Gardening clothes should be comfortable and old. It's a good idea to wear cotton shirts with long sleeves to shade your arms from the sun and to protect them from getting scratched by plants with sharp thorns. Long trousers are also safer, although on hot days you can wear shorts as long as you remember to put sunscreen on your legs. You may need an old cushion or a rubber kneeling pad or you will end up with very muddy knees.

After a long day in the garden have a soapy soak in your bathtub. Your muscles will be tired after all that bending, and your hands and knees will come clean with a good scrubbing.

ON YOUR HEAD

A hat is probably your most important item of clothing. It's best to wear one with a wide brim to shade the back of your neck because gardening involves a lot of kneeling down or bending over. Those peaked hats with a flap at the back are also very good.

GARDENING WITH KIDS

Gardening is all about having fun and staying safe, which means you need to be dressed in the right clothes and be aware of a few basic precautions before you go outside and start digging.

ON YOUR HANDS

Gardening gloves are perfect for certain tasks, although they can be a nuisance when you are doing fiddly jobs such as planting tiny seeds or small seedlings. Always wear gloves when weeding because you never know what insects may be hiding at ground level. It's not much fun being bitten by an ant or a spider, and your gloves will certainly protect you.

on your feet

Gumboots will keep your feet dry even when the ground is soaking wet. Wear thick, comfortable socks inside your boots and remember to always shake them well each time you put them on because spiders and other insects occasionally crawl inside boots that have been left on a verandah or in the shed. There are handy wooden racks with rods for hanging boots upside down – these can be positioned near the back door so you get into the habit of putting on your boots every time you venture into the garden. Although it's lovely to walk barefoot on the soft grass, remember that most people who are bitten by bees have accidentally stepped on them.

caring for tools

Look after your garden tools by storing them under cover. You can have your own special place for keeping your tools together. Hand tools are easy to lose so pick ones with brightly coloured handles that can be easily seen when you are packing up after working in the garden. Never leave long handled tools like rakes or hoes lying on the grass. You can easily step on the wrong end and the handle will flip up and conk you on the head. I've made that mistake a few times!

getting into the garden The best time of day for gardening in the summer is the early morning, straight after breakfast. Once the sun has risen in the sky it will be too hot for gardening, except in shady areas. In spring and autumn you can work in the garden for longer periods because the weather is not so extreme. In winter it's good to start gardening mid morning when the sun has warmed the soil a little. Make sure you are warmly dressed on those chilly winter days.

BRING IN THE BIRDS

Encourage birds into the garden with a birdbath or feeding table. Birds are not just beautiful but helpful because they love eating insects that may be damaging your plants. If you have cats it's definitely not a good idea to hang a bird feeder where they can stalk and catch our feathered friends.

Take a bottle of water and some fruit into the garden and have regular breaks. In summer you should stop and have a cool drink every half an hour, and remember that fruit has natural sugars that will give you an energy boost.

keeping chooks

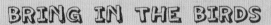

If you have a large enough garden consider a portable run so you can keep a couple of chickens. They will provide some rich manure for the garden and, of course, some fresh organic eggs. Chickens love to free range around the garden but they can cause a bit of damage and mess by digging up seedlings and scratching the mulch onto the lawn. It's best to keep the chickens in their cage until towards the end of summer when plants are well established. Chickens will certainly help to keep unwanted insects under control if you allow them to scratch around.

my garden tools

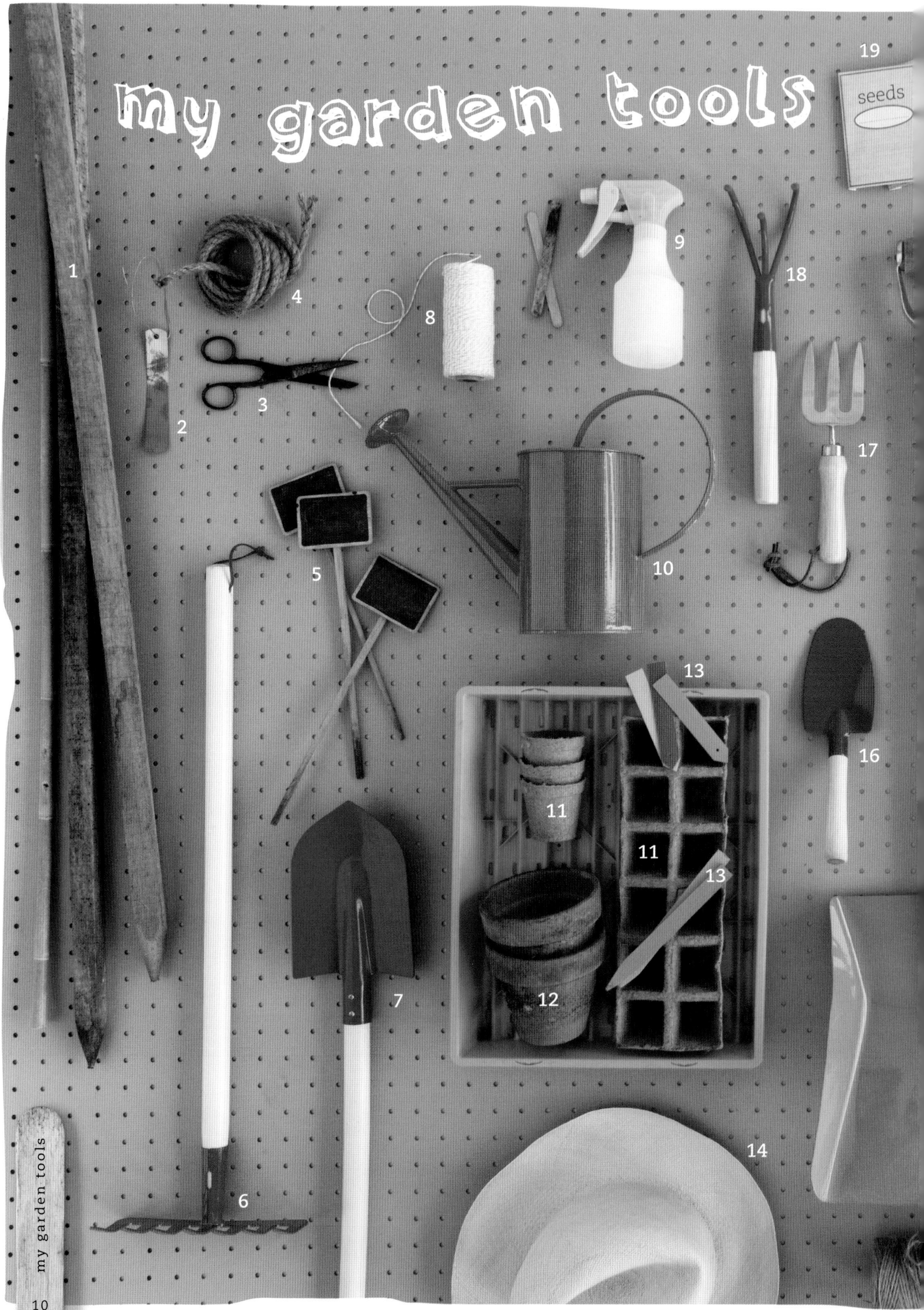

1

2

3

4

5

6

7

8

9

10

11

11

12

13

13

14

16

17

18

19 seeds

The tools you choose for the garden should be the right size for your height and age, and they will last for years if you look after them properly. You don't need a large number of tools, just a basic set that can be used for a wide range of different jobs.

A good sharp spade with a wooden handle is probably your most important tool. The handle should be rubbed with sandpaper once a year and then apply some linseed oil to keep the handle from drying out and cracking. This job is best done in winter when you are not using your tools every day.

A basic tool kit will consist of a spade, a fork and a hoe that is used for chipping out weeds. Then you will need some hand tools including a small trowel, a hand cultivator and hand fork. The long handled tools are for tackling the big jobs, and the hand tools are for when you are kneeling down doing the more delicate tasks. An old blunt kitchen knife is also a good tool to keep in your kit. It is excellent for weeding around small seedlings without damaging them.

Wash the dirt off your garden tools every time you have finished working, then wipe the blades dry with an old cloth. Store them in a dry place and they will be ready for you the next time you head for the garden.

1 Wooden stakes 2 Plant ID tags
3 Gardening scissors 4 Rope 5 Plant ID tags
6 Rake 7 Spade 8 Garden string 9 Spray bottle 10 Watering can 11 Disintegrating pots 12 Terracotta pots 13 Plant ID tags
14 Sun hat 15 Square shovel 16 Trowel
17 Hand fork 18 Hand cultivator
19 Seed packets 20 Plastic rake
21 Hoe 22 Gumboots 23 Plant ID tags
24 Plastic pots 25 Secateurs
26 Gardening gloves 27 Bucket

my garden tools

my first garden

egg man

step two Fill each egg shell with a ball of cotton wool and sprinkle the tiny seeds of alfalfa on the top. Gently pour 2 tablespoons of water onto the cotton wool.

step one Save egg shells to use as mini holders for sprouting alfalfa seeds. Decorate them with colourful acrylic paint and allow the paint to dry upside down for an hour.

step three Keep the egg men in a light, bright position but not in direct sunlight. Depending on the room temperature, the seeds will sprout after five days or more. It's fun to watch the tiny green shoots appear like magic!

mung beans

step two Leave the beans to soak for 5 minutes then tip all the water out of the jar. Place the jar in a light, bright place but not in direct sunlight. Repeat the process of rinsing the beans with water two or three times a day.

step one In a clear glass jar place 2 tablespoons of unsprouted mung beans and fill the jar with water. Cover the top of the jar with muslin and tie with string.

step three After 4 or 5 days the beans should start to produce crisp sprouts. It takes a little longer when the weather is cool. It's important that the beans are not allowed to dry out or they may not produce sprouts. After sprouting keep them in the fridge, and start a fresh batch.

how to grow

Gardening is very easy once you understand the basic ideas. There really are no strict rules to follow. It's more about enjoying yourself, and using a little old-fashioned common sense.

getting started

Plants need good soil, plenty of sunshine and regular rainfall to grow strong and healthy. It's a fact that plants grown in the best possible conditions will not only produce more flowers and fruit, they will be able to fight off attack by pests and diseases. They will be tough, and resilient. However, weak plants that are struggling to survive because the soil is bad or because they have not been watered during dry weather, will be more likely to experience all sorts of problems. So our main aim in being good gardeners is to start by preparing the soil before we even begin to think about planting.

soil testing

Depending on where you live your soil will be heavy (clay); medium (friable); or light (sandy). It's easy to test your soil to discover what type it is. Simply dig a hole in the ground, to a depth of about 30cm (12 inches). Examine the soil from the hole and see if it is sticky (clay); crumbly (friable) or sandy (light).

Fill the hole with water and see how long it takes to drain away. If it stays in the hole for more than 20 minutes the soil probably has too much clay content. If the water drains away in a matter of minutes it means that your soil is probably too sandy.

organic matter

Digging in or layering the surface with what we call 'organic matter' will effectively improve all three types of soil. Manures and composts are known as organic matter or soil-builders and they are the secret of any successful garden. You will be amazed at the improvement in the soil after these soil-builders have been added. It will be time to start planting!

glorious sunshine

A few plant varieties prefer to be grown in the shade, but in general most need at least five or six hours of sunshine a day to produce flowers or fruit. Vegetable and herb gardens, in particular, should always be positioned in an open, sunny place and well away from large trees that have spreading root systems. These tree roots will rob the soil of moisture and nutrients, which means that the plants you are trying to grow will struggle to survive. There will simply be too much competition. So look for a sunny spot that has plenty of space around when planning your first garden bed.

did you know?

When you open a bag of potting mix, bacteria- and fungi-producing spores are released into the air you breathe. For this reason, it's important to step back or walk away from the bag for a few minutes until they have dispersed. As an extra precaution, you could wear a mask. And of course, always wear gardening gloves when handling potting mix.

magical mulches

When you have planted out your garden, the next important step is to mulch around the plants to help keep the weeds from growing back and to stop the soil from drying out too quickly after watering. A mulch layer is like an insulating blanket on the surface of the soil. It needs to be about 7-10cm (3-4 inches) in depth. Always leave a little space around the base of plants because if the mulch layer is pushing against the stem it can smother the plant or create very humid conditions that can actually kill the plant. It's good to also mulch around trees and shrubs to keep weeds or lawn from growing too close to the trunk of the plant.

which mulch?

The best mulches are natural materials such as lucerne straw, hay, home made compost, animals manures, grass clippings, leaves, bark chips and pine bark. These will eventually break down into the soil and help to keep it healthy. You can buy mulches from a plant nursery or you can make your own compost and save up the grass clippings. In autumn rake all the leaves into a pile and let them rot down. They make marvellous mulch in the summer vegetable garden.

marvellous manures Animals are a gardener's best friend. Not animals that come in and eat the roses or trample on the seedlings, but animals that provide the manure that is essential for rich, healthy soil. The most common soil improvers used in the garden are cow, horse and poultry manures. These can be bought in bags from a garden nursery, or they can be picked up in bulk by the trailer load from a landscape supply yard. Sheep and goat manure is also very useful, but not as easy to find. Sometimes farmers put sheep manure into bags and put them at the front gate. You often see these bags for sale when you are on a drive in the country. You must remember, however, that manure has a very strong smell, especially when it's fresh. Some people think it's a horrible smell, but most gardeners don't mind the pongy aromas because they know it means that soon their soil will be rich and fertile. It's best not to use very fresh manure because it can burn the roots of plants. Manure that has been bought from a nursery or landscape yard will already have been 'aged' and is therefore quite safe to dig into the ground before planting. However if you are using manure directly from a farm or from your own backyard chickens, pile it in one corner of the garden and let it 'rot down' for a few months before using it.

Plants prefer to be given a long soaking drink of water than just a light sprinkling. Soak each plant so that the soil around it is completely damp and this will encourage the plant roots to travel down deeply into the ground, in turn making the plant stronger. This also means that you will need to water much less often, especially if the ground around the plant has been mulched.

wonderful water

Ideally, plants should be able to grow happily from regular rainfall. However in most climates extra watering is needed to keep them growing strongly, especially in summer. Care must be taken not to waste any water, as this is such a precious resource. So don't splash water around on the paths or lawn, instead direct it only where it is most needed, around the base of plants. You can use a sprinkler or you can water using the hose and a sprinkling nozzle. Check to make sure there are no watering restrictions and only water the garden in the early morning or the late afternoon. Watering in the middle of the day in summer is a waste of time because the water simply evaporates in the heat.

planting trees and shrubs

When you buy trees and shrubs from the nursery they will be in pots, and often the roots inside these pots will be a bit overcrowded or tangled. So make sure you dig a big hole that is about twice the size of the pot (and the roots). Mix the soil from the hole with some compost or well-rotted manure and use this underneath the plant and again to fill in around the plant. If the roots are very tangled it helps to gently tease them out before planting, so that they can then quickly start spreading out into the lovely soil you have provided for them. Don't forget to water immediately after planting, and then mulch around the tree or shrub to keep the ground from drying out.

seeds

Seeds need moisture and warmth to sprout, and you must provide these conditions to successfully get them to germinate. It also helps to use the right soil mix, which must be light and yet still able to hold moisture. Special seed raising mixes are available from plant nurseries.

step one Fill a shallow tray – make sure the tray has drainage holes – with seed raising mixture, to a depth of at least 8-10cm (3-4 inches). This will allow enough room for the seedlings to develop strong, downward growing roots.

step two Level the seed raising mix with a rake or hoe to create a smooth and even surface for positioning the seeds. Press down lightly so the soil mix is firm.

step three Place the seeds on the surface of the soil mixture, leaving at least 2-3 cm (1 inch) between each seed. This will make it easier to separate them for transplanting.

Growing plants from seed is one of the cheapest and easiest ways of creating a new garden. It takes a little longer because you have to allow time for the seeds to germinate and grow large enough for you to transplant them out into the soil. However, it's a lot of fun and very satisfying to know that you have cared for your plants from the seed stage right through to flowering.

step five Water lightly. Most seeds like to be kept lightly moist until they have germinated, but again check on the seed packet. Bean seeds, for example, can rot underground if the soil mix is overwatered.

step four Cover the seeds with an extra 1cm (½ inch) of soil mixture and pat down lightly with your hand to make sure the seeds are firmly in place. Larger seeds may need to be covered with more soil mix – check planting depth on the seed packet.

step six When the seedlings are 8-10cm (3-4 inches) tall they can be lifted and transplanted into the garden. Handle them with care, making sure not to damage the roots as you separate the plants from each other.

cuttings

One of the greatest adventures in gardening is creating your own new plants. It's a process that is called propagation.

What propagation means is that you can simply cut a small section from a mature plant and use it to produce a new one. Most shrubby plants have stems that can be cut with secateurs and trimmed into mini plants that are capable of growing their own roots. These are called cuttings, and in time they will grow into shrubs that are as big and beautiful as the original plant from which the little stem was cut.

Beginners should try cuttings of fuchsia, geranium, hydrangea, rosemary, chrysanthemum and daphne. These are all common shrubs that you will find in your friends', or neighbours' gardens and you will be surprised at how easy it is to grow them from cuttings.

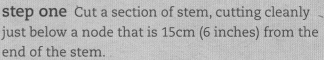

step one Cut a section of stem, cutting cleanly just below a node that is 15cm (6 inches) from the end of the stem.

step two Trim the top of the cutting by removing any leaves that are low down on the cutting, and cutting back leaves at the top. The finished cutting should be about 10cm (4 inches) in length.

step three Insert the lower end of the cutting into a small container of potting mix, firming down well. Water in.

seedlings

A fast way of growing flowering annuals or vegetables is to buy seedlings that are at the stage when they are just ready to transplant.

It's a good idea to transplant your seedlings as quickly as you can when you get them home from the nursery. If you leave them sitting around too long they will dry out and die, or the roots will become very dense from sitting in the punnet. Get the soil ready first, then buy your seedlings and transplant them as soon as possible.

Seedlings are sold in plant nurseries in plastic punnets that make it easy for them to be separated and planted out into soil that has been prepared in advance. Look for healthy seedlings that are not overgrown or overcrowded as these will produce much better results.

step one Tip the seedlings from the punnet into your hand, then gently separate them taking care not to damage roots that are tangled together.
step two Don't plant them too close to each other and keep the soil at the same level as in the punnet. They don't like being planted too deeply.
step three Water them in and after a few days, mulch around them with some lucerne straw.

Compost is a rich mixture of organic matter
that is tossed together and allowed to rot down
to produce a nutrient-rich material that can be
added to garden beds. Save all the vegetable
peelings and scraps from the kitchen and mix
them up with grass clippings and leaves from
the garden to make wonderful rich compost
that will improve the quality of the soil and
make your plants stronger and healthier.

the compost bin

wonderful worms

Worms multiply naturally in healthy soil. It is also possible to 'farm' worms that will produce liquids and solids that are fantastic plant fertilisers.

worm farming

Worm farming is fun, and easy-to-manage kits can be set up outside and used to recycle kitchen scraps as an alternative to composting. Some local councils will provide worm farms for city gardeners to encourage them to recycle rather than discard organic waste. Carefully follow the instructions provided with your worm farm kit and you will get fantastic results. Pay particular attention to the amount of water you use. Too much water can drown the worms.

how worm farms work

Worm farms work quite simply. The worms are fed with anything organic from vegetable and fruit peelings to tea leaves and crushed egg shells, and afterwards the solids (castings) and liquids they discard are used as plant fertilisers. Worm farms should be placed in a shady place as they like a cool, protected environment.

step one Open the worm farm and prepare a bed of garden soil and shredded newspaper in the upper chamber. Water lightly.
step two Add 1,000-2,000 worms and watch them burrow into their moist bedding.
step three Feed the worms daily with chopped up organic matter and make sure the farm is always moist (not wet). The liquid and casting will drop through to the lower chamber.

step four Dilute the worm farm liquid in water (ratio of 1:5) and use as a liquid fertiliser. Mix the casting into the soil before planting.

the herb garden

Fresh herbs add fantastic flavour to everything you cook and the good news is that they are very easy to grow in any sunny part of the garden and most don't need a lot of watering.

dill

coriander

tarragon

basil

rosemary

mint

bay

oregano

chervil

spearmint

parsley

thyme

sage

purple cress

marjoram

watercress

thai basil

chives

growing herbs

Spring is the best season to get your herb garden started. Most garden nurseries have a good selection of potted herbs, and you can select your favourites and bring them home once the garden bed has been prepared.

herb history

Herbs are simply fragrant, flavour plants that are edible and have been used for hundreds of years to add extra taste to the food of every country around the world.

Many of the most popular herbs come from the Mediterranean regions of Europe but we also love to cook with herbs and spices from India, Southeast Asia, the Middle East and South America. Some herbs can also be made into medicinal plants, and their strong fragrance means that they are also used for making soaps and bath oils and other aromatic products.

landscaping with herbs

Some herbs are shrubby plants, such as rosemary and sage; some are trees, such as bay; some are perennial plants such as oregano, marjoram and thyme; and some are annuals, such as basil and coriander. You can plant them all together in a special area of the garden – creating a lovely aromatic herb bed. Or you can grow them in and around other flowering ornamental plants, such as roses or lavender, because they have lovely foliage and this makes them useful as general garden plants (as well as being useful for cooking). When planting a herb garden place the taller growing plants (bay, rosemary, sage) towards the back of the garden then place the medium and smaller herbs towards the front. Thyme and oregano make a lovely front border.

what herbs need

All herbs like to be grown in an area of the garden that gets at least 4-6 hours of sunshine a day. They like medium to light (sandy) soil that has good drainage. This means that when it's been raining or the garden has been watered, the soil is capable of allowing excess moisture to drain away rather that collecting around the roots of the plants. Gardeners say that herbs 'don't like having wet feet' and this really tells you the conditions that must be created to keep them growing strong and healthy. So if you live in an area where the soil is thick clay, you will need to dig lots of compost into the garden bed before planting. Most herbs don't need to be watered all the time and they also don't require a lot of fertiliser or manure.

raised herb beds

It's also possible to improve the soil drainage by building up a garden bed especially for growing herbs. Use rocks, bricks or railway sleepers as an edging and then put in barrow loads of your own compost or bags of good garden mix from the nursery, mixed together with your own soil. This will make a perfect environment for planting out your herbs.

herbs in pots

Herbs also enjoy being grown in containers. Terracotta pots create a wonderful environment for planting herbs because they are porous which means the soil doesn't stay too damp after watering. You can also get troughs that are ideal for growing three or four different herbs together, and these can be positioned on a sunny kitchen windowsill so that the herbs are handy for picking whenever you are cooking.

the herb garden

32

chives

Chives are the smallest member of the onion family, also called alliums, and are related to garlic, leeks and spring onions. They can be easily grown from seed, creating a small clump of grassy foliage topped by pretty pink to mauve flower heads.

about chives

Chives are found growing wild around the countryside in Europe. They have long, dark green leaves that are hollow, and round clusters of tiny pink flowers on top of slender stems. Both the foliage and the flowers of chives can be eaten, and they have been used as culinary plants for thousands of years.

growing chives

Chives are perennial plants, which means that the clumps will die back in the winter and pop up again the following spring with new foliage and flowers. So choose a place in the garden where they can have a permanent home or grow them in a pot placed in a sunny position. Chives need more watering than most herbs, especially during hot, dry summers. They will grow easily in most soils, and they can either be germinated from seeds or bought in small pots and transplanted directly into the garden.

using chives

Cut small bunches of chives as you need them, using sharp scissors. They can then be chopped up and used in salads or as a flavouring in soups and stews. They are particularly good chopped up in mashed potatoes or sprinkled over the top of poached or scrambled eggs. They also go well with fish. The good thing about chives is that they have that distinctive onion flavour, but much milder, which is why kids often love them. Chives can be chopped up and dried on a paper towel in a dry place, then stored in jars for use in cooking. Keep the dried herbs in a dark place.

did you know?

Chives have an onion aroma that is good for repelling insects. So plant them in the vegetable patch. Also, because their flowers are a pink colour they attract bees, which is great for those plants in your garden that need pollinating (e.g. apple and plum trees).

parsley

Parsley is the world's most popular herb, and no garden should be without a clump of this bright green plant which is rich in vitamins A and C.

about parsley

Parsley is a native herb of Italy and Tunisia where it can be seen growing wild in fields and rocky mountain slopes. It is valued for its foliage which can be deep green and crinkled in appearance (curly parsley) or with paler green, flat leaves (called flat-leaf or Italian parsley). Flat-leaf parsley has a much stronger flavour.

growing parsley

Parsley is a biennial plant, which means that it keeps growing for nearly two years. The seeds are tiny and take a long time to germinate, so it's easier and faster to buy seedlings. If you plant parsley in the spring it will quickly thrive and produce foliage for eating in just a few weeks. It will continue to grow vigorously, and then it will slow down in winter. In cold climates it almost disappears then grows back the following spring. By mid summer it will start to produce flowers and after that it will die back completely. So if you want to have

parsley in the garden all year round, plant new seeds or seedlings every spring and enjoy a constant supply.

using parsley

Parsley is chopped finely and used as a garnish or flavouring in soups, stews and salads. It goes well with vegetables and with meat or fish. In the Middle East they make a tabbouleh salad (opposite). In Italy they mix parsley, garlic and grated lemon rind together to make gremolata, which is added to veal stew as it is served. Delicious!

did you know?

Parsley is a valuable companion plant, which means it can be used to benefit other plants in the herb or vegetable garden by attracting wasps and other insects, which in turn eat smaller insects. In the old days parsley was believed to have magical powers.

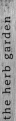

the herb garden

tabbouleh

¼ cup (40g) burghul
3 medium tomatoes (450g)
3 cups coarsely chopped fresh
   flat-leaf parsley
3 green onions (scallions),
   chopped finely
½ cup coarsely chopped fresh mint
1 clove garlic, crushed
¼ cup (60ml) lemon juice
¼ cup (60ml) olive oil

1 Place the burghul in a shallow
medium bowl. Cut the tomatoes in
half; use a teaspoon to scoop seeds
from tomato over the burghul. Chop
the tomato flesh finely; spread over
burghul. Cover; refrigerate 1 hour or
until burghul is swollen and tender.
2 Put the burghul mixture in a large
bowl with the rest of the ingredients,
season to taste; mix well.
prep time 30 minutes (+ refrigeration)
serves 4
nutritional count per serving 14.2g
total fat (2g saturated fat); 790kJ (189 cal);
9.4g carbohydrate; 3.6g protein; 5.9g fibre

NOTES Perfect tabbouleh relies on perfect
parsley. Make sure that the parsley is washed to
remove any grit and dried well before adding to
the salad. If the parsley is too wet, you will find
that your tabbouleh turns a little mushy, rather
than being light and tasty. Use a salad spinner
(if you have one) to dry the washed parsley or
pat it dry with absorbent paper. This recipe
seems like a lot of chopping but to save time
use a pair of kitchen scissors to chop the herbs
and green onions.
Serve the tabbouleh with felafel and pitta bread.

Sage

Sage is a pretty, bushy plant with aromatic grey/green foliage and blue/purple flowers. It looks attractive growing in any part of the garden – not just in the herb patch.

about sage

Sage is a small, evergreen shrub, which means you can pick and use the leaves all year round. Although originally a wild plant in Europe, it has been cultivated since medieval times and the leaves have a slightly peppery flavour. It has been used not just as a culinary herb, but also as a medicinal plant for a wide range of illnesses.

growing sage

Sage is a very easy shrub to grow because it's not particularly fussy about soil and it doesn't require a lot of watering, even in summer. However good drainage is important, so add lots of compost to the planting hole if your soil is heavy clay. Choose a lovely sunny part of the garden or place it near a verandah or outdoor living area because the foliage exudes a pleasant fragrance. After flowering you can prune the shrub back to stop it from getting straggly. The leaves from the pruned stems can be dried and stored in jars for up to 12 months.

using sage

Sage is one of the four most popular herbs (parsley, sage, rosemary and thyme) used for making stuffing for chicken, pork or turkey and also for sausages. It's often used to make up a bouquet garni, which is a small bundle of mixed herbs used to flavour stews and casseroles. It can also be made into a soothing tea, which can be sweetened with a teaspoon of honey.

did you know?

The botanical name for sage is *Salvia* which is derived from a Latin word which meant 'to save' because in ancient times the plant was believed to have magical qualities. They thought it could ward off evil, protect from snakebites and help people live longer.

the herb garden

oregano

Oregano is related to the herb marjoram, which has similar growing requirements and a slightly different flavour. There are lots of different varieties of oregano, including one with brilliant golden leaves that makes a very pretty ornamental plant on the edge of a flower border.

about oregano

Oregano is a perennial, which means that once planted in the garden it will keep producing foliage for you to harvest year after year. It was originally found growing wild in Europe and parts of Asia and has become very popular in Italian and Greek cooking. All parts of the plant can be used, even the seeds, and the leaves are also used to extract an aromatic oil.

growing oregano

Oregano will do well in full sun or partial shade and can be grown in a wide range of soils and climates, making it a versatile plant that will suit most gardens. It can also be grown in a container, which looks very pretty as it will cascade over the sides. After flowering, prune the plant back and save the prunings because they can be dried and stored in jars for cooking. The dried leaves have a stronger flavour than when the plant is used fresh.

using oregano

Italian recipes often call for oregano, especially pasta sauces and pizzas. You can place a stem of oregano in a bottle of olive oil and it will give it a lovely flavour for making salad dressings. It goes well as a garnish in a fresh tomato salad and the leaves can also be made into a tea which is good to drink if you have a cold.

did you know?

The essential oil made from oregano is often used in perfumes designed for men and, many years ago, it was also used to kill head lice. Plant breeders have recently produced a variety of oregano called 'Hot and Spicy' which has a much more intense, peppery flavour.

You can learn to tell the difference between the herbs just from the way they smell. Crush the leaves between your fingers to bring out the strongest aromas.

coriander

Coriander, also called cilantro, is a leafy green herb with a distinctive and rather intense aroma and flavour that people either love or hate. The whole plant (including the roots and stem) is used in Asian cooking.

about coriander

Coriander is an annual plant, which means that it can only be grown for one season. You will need to plant fresh seeds or seedlings every spring. It is a native plant of southern Europe, north Africa and parts of Asia and has become one of the most popular herbs in modern cuisine. It's a very pretty plant with fresh, green fragrant foliage and seeds that also can be collected and used in cooking.

growing coriander

Coriander must have warm to hot growing conditions and plenty of water to keep it producing lots of lush foliage for harvesting. One problem is that it's inclined to produce flowers and seed heads very quickly, after which the foliage dies back. So make sure you pinch out any stems that look like they could be about to flower. However if you also want to collect the seeds, set aside a couple of plants just for this purpose. Coriander likes plenty of sun and can be grown just as well in a pot as directly in the ground.

using coriander

Coriander is often used as a fresh herb in Asian and Middle Eastern recipes. Finely chopped coriander is also used as a garnish on salsa and guacamole. The seeds can be saved and used in spicy curries to add a special flavour. The seeds have a very different aroma and flavour from the fresh leaves.

did you know?

If you plant coriander near roses it will help to prevent the rosebuds being attacked by sap-sucking little aphids. This is because the coriander has such a strong smell it throws these tiny insects into a state of confusion.

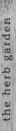

the herb garden

coriander chicken kebabs with pesto

1 teaspoon each coriander seeds and
   cumin seeds
1 teaspoon sea salt
750g (1½ pounds) chicken breast fillets,
   cut into 2.5cm (1-inch) pieces
1 tablespoon cornflour (cornstarch)
1 cup firmly packed fresh coriander
   (cilantro) leaves
2 cloves garlic, quartered
¼ cup (25g) walnuts, roasted
1 tablespoon finely grated
   parmesan cheese
1 teaspoon lemon juice
⅓ cup (60ml) olive oil

1 Cook the coriander seeds, cumin seeds
and salt in a small frying pan, over low
heat, stirring with a wooden spoon, until
you can smell the spices. Put the spice
mixture into a mortar and pestle and
crush it until it is finely ground.
2 Put the chicken, spice mixture and
cornflour in a medium bowl; mix well.
Thread chicken onto 12 skewers; cook
skewers on a heated oiled grill plate (or
grill or barbecue), turning with tongs until
chicken is cooked through.
3 Meanwhile, put the coriander leaves,
garlic, nuts, cheese and juice in a blender
or food processor; blend or process until
the ingredients are combined. With motor
operating on low speed, slowly add the oil,
in a thin steady stream; process until pesto
is smooth. Season to taste.
4 Serve skewers with coriander pesto.
prep + cook time 40 minutes **makes** 12
nutritional count per kebab 8.7g total fat
(1.6g saturated fat); 513kJ (123 cal); 0.7g
carbohydrate; 10.5g protein; 0.3g fibre

TIPS If you don't have a mortar and pestle you
can grind the spice mixture in a small food processor.
We used metal skewers for this recipe. If you are using
bamboo skewers you will need to soak them in cold
water for at least 30 minutes before using. This stops
them burning during cooking.

rosemary

Rosemary is a herb rich in fragrant oils and it's one of the most widely used of all aromatic plants, both for cooking and in the cosmetics industry.

about rosemary

Rosemary is a woody perennial plant that grows into a large, spreading bush covered with needle-like olive green foliage and stems topped with light blue flowers in the spring time. There are also varieties with purple and pink flowers. It is a symbol of friendship, loyalty and remembrance and a sprig of rosemary is worn on the day we hold services to remember soldiers who have died in war. It's an excellent ornamental plant for any sunny, protected part of the garden and it can also be planted as a hedge and kept trimmed into a neat shape.

growing rosemary

Rosemary is a very easy plant to grow although it has some specific requirements. It likes warmth and well-drained soil and sometimes even a large, healthy bush will die suddenly if there is a cold, wet winter. So choose a sunny position and dig plenty of compost into the planting hole if your soil is heavy clay. Keep the bush well trimmed, cutting it back after spring flowering, and save all the prunings for drying and storing in jars.

using rosemary

Rosemary has a very strong aroma and flavour and is used with roasted meats, especially lamb and veal. It also goes well with vegetables, and needs to be chopped very finely because the leaves are tough and have a slightly bitter taste. Sprigs of rosemary can be put into bottles of olive oil or vinegar for making delicious salad dressings.

did you know?

In ancient Greece rosemary was believed to improve people's memory, and students would wear garlands of rosemary around their necks when they were sitting for exams. You can soak rosemary in boiling water and allow to cool, then use it as a rinse after you have shampooed your hair. It will smell wonderful.

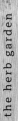

lamb cutlets in barbecue sauce and rosemary

12 french-trimmed lamb cutlets (880g)
½ cup (125ml) barbecue sauce
2 tablespoons finely chopped
  fresh rosemary
2 cloves garlic, crushed
2 tablespoons olive oil
400g (12½ ounces) green beans, trimmed

1 Place the cutlets in a shallow dish.
Put the sauce, rosemary, garlic and oil
in a small jug and mix well; pour sauce
mixture over the cutlets.
2 Cook cutlets on a heated oiled grill plate
(or grill or barbecue), turning with tongs.
3 Meanwhile, boil, steam or microwave
beans until tender; drain.
4 Serve cutlets with beans; season to taste.
prep + cook time 15 minutes **serves** 4
nutritional count per serving 28.2g total
fat (9.9g saturated fat); 1793kJ (429 cal);
18.2g carbohydrate; 24.7g protein; 3.3g fibre

TIP To remove rosemary leaves from
the stalk hold one end of the stalk in one
hand; run the fingertips from your other
hand down the length of the stalk, pulling
the leaves off as you go.

thyme

There are dozens of different varieties of thyme, each with their own particular fragrance and flavour. It's a rather straggly-looking little plant, but it can look very pretty growing in a pot, especially when it is flowering.

about thyme

Thyme is an ancient plant and there are records of it being used both as a culinary herb and for medicinal purposes thousands of years ago. It's called a 'shrublet' because it's a very small woody plant and the foliage is tiny and carried on small stems from the main branches. Once your thyme plants have established they should last for years and years, and you can harvest the leaves all year round or pick them when growth is lush in summer, and dry them for storing and using later.

using thyme

Thyme is used in many different styles of cooking to flavour soups, marinades, stuffings and roasted vegetables. It is often used in the oil that preserves olives and it goes well with lamb, tomatoes and eggs. It keeps its flavour, even in recipes that are slow cooked, and is just as useful fresh as dried.

did you know?

In ancient times the herb thyme was associated with death, probably because the Egyptians used it when embalming mummies. The oil extracted from thyme was also used as an antiseptic and even modern practitioners use it in the practice of aromatherapy.

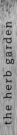

bay tree

Bay is one of the few herbs that is a tree, and a very large tree indeed if it is not kept clipped back on a regular basis. In fact, it can also be used for topiary, which is where trees or shrubs are clipped into a particular shape.

about bay
Also known by the name laurel, the bay tree has bright green leathery leaves, which are harvested and then dried to produce a brittle grey-green herb that has a slightly bitter taste. Bay is a native tree of the Mediterranean regions of Europe, and has been used as a culinary and medicinal herb for more than a thousand years.

growing bay
Ideally bay trees prefer a climate that has mild, wet winters and hot dry summers, however they are quite adaptable trees and can be seen growing strongly in a wide range of climates from very cold to sub-tropical. They like a sunny position and soil that is well drained. The tree can be kept quite small by regularly removing the young branches and stems as they shoot upwards in summer. These should be hung up to dry and the leaves stored in airtight containers.

using bay leaves
Bay is one of the main ingredients of bouquet garni – a bunch of mixed dried herbs that are used for flavouring stews, soups and sauces. A bay leaf is often added to the water used for boiling meats, such as corned beef and is also an important ingredient in pea soup. The dried leaves will keep their flavour for about a year, but a single tree will provide you with much more than you will need – you will be giving branches to friends and family.

did you know?
In ancient Greece athletes were given laurel wreaths as a prize for winning events in the Olympic Games. A wreath is simply a stem of the young bay tree, tied in a circle and worn on the head.

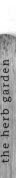

the herb garden

mint

There are many different varieties of mint, with lots of different leaf shapes and flavours. It is one of the easiest of all herbs to grow and can be used in many different recipes.

about mint

The mints are part of a large family of herbs that have been used in cooking for more than a thousand years. They are fast growing, perennial plants that spread by sending out stems that produce strong roots, so you will find your mint plants can invade garden beds and become a nuisance unless kept under control.

growing mint

Mint likes a sunny position and must have plenty of water in the summer. A lot of people plant a clump of mint under a garden tap, because they get a bit of extra watering every time the tap is turned on. Mint seems to thrive in most soils and climates, and it will die back in the winter and burst back to life in spring, especially in colder climates.

using mint

Mint has a strong menthol flavour, although there are so many different varieties that each have a particular taste, such as spearmint and peppermint. All of them are used extensively in cooking. Mint sauce is often served with lamb and mint also goes very well with fresh tomatoes. Mint can also be made into a refreshing tea.

did you know?

If you plant mint near the back door of your house it will help keep ants from coming inside. Mint can also be crushed and used to repel mosquitoes and in ancient Greece crushed mint was sprinkled on the floor as a room deodoriser.

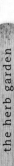

the herb garden

minted melon salad

½ small rockmelon (650g)
1 small honeydew melon (1.3kg)
1kg (2-pound) piece seedless watermelon
¼ cup loosely packed fresh mint leaves
½ cup (125ml) apple juice

1 Use a spoon to scoop the seeds from the rockmelon and honeydew; throw the seeds away. Using a melon baller, scoop balls from the rockmelon and honeydew and put them into a large bowl.
2 Chop watermelon into small chunks, add to the bowl. Stir in the mint and juice.
prep time 20 minutes **serves** 8
nutritional count per serving 0.6g total fat (0g saturated fat); 326kJ (78 cal); 15.7g carbohydrate; 1.3g protein; 2.2g fibre

TIP You can use any combination of melons or other fruit you like.

basil

Basil has become one of the most popular herbs in cooking and is available in green or purple varieties. Its fresh leaves are best used as soon as you pick them, or they will start to lose their flavour.

about basil

Basil is an annual herb that is grown from seed or seedlings planted in the spring and harvested right through until the autumn. There are dozens of different varieties of basil, from many regions of the world including Europe, Africa and Asia. The most commonly used basil is the one known as 'sweet basil'.

growing basil

Basil needs a warm summer to grow well, and should be positioned in a semi-shaded position to help prevent it from quickly producing flowering stems. Basil grows extremely well in pots on a protected window sill and you can keep it producing foliage for much longer if you pinch out any flower stems as soon as they appear. Regular harvesting will encourage the plants to be bushier.

using basil

Basil is used a lot in Italian cooking, but is also a popular herb for Asian cuisine. It goes particularly well with tomatoes, and is also used to flavour pasta sauces and vegetables. Crushed basil with garlic is called pistou and added as a flavouring to soups.

did you know?

In India, basil is considered to be a sacred plant as it is often seen growing in the grounds of temples. In Asia, basil was traditionally used to treat snake bite (however do not try this at home!).

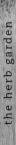

the herb garden

cos salad with basil dressing

4 rindless bacon slices (260g),
   sliced thinly
3 baby cos (romaine) lettuce, trimmed,
   leaves separated
basil dressing
⅓ cup each firmly packed fresh basil
   leaves and flat-leaf parsley leaves
¼ cup (60ml) white wine vinegar
¼ cup (60ml) olive oil
1 tablespoon wholegrain mustard
3 ice cubes

1 Make basil dressing.
2 Cook the bacon in a heated oiled
large frying pan, stirring with a wooden
spoon, until crisp. Remove bacon from
the pan with a slotted spoon and drain
on absorbent paper.
3 Arrange the lettuce leaves in a large
bowl, sprinkle with the bacon. Serve the
salad drizzled with the dressing.
basil dressing Put all of the ingredients
in a blender or food processor; blend or
process until the dressing is smooth.
Season to taste.
prep + cook time 15 minutes **serves** 8
nutritional count per serving 9.9g total
fat (2g saturated fat); 543kJ (130 cal);
1.5g carbohydrate; 7.7g protein; 1.6g fibre

TIP The ice cubes will "hold" the
bright green colour in the dressing and
stop it turning brown.

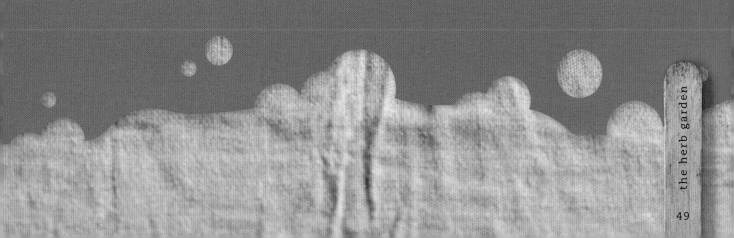

lavender sachets

The dried flowers of lavender have a wonderful fragrance that will make the clothes in your drawers smell sweet for more than a year.

step one When the lavender bushes are in full flower, pick the blooms and take enough stem so that they can be tied for drying. The plants benefit from the flowers being picked as they will produce even more flowers the next season.

step two Use a length of string to tie the lavender flowers together in bunches. It's better to make three or four bunches as they will dry more evenly than if you bundle them together in one very large bunch.

step three Cover each bunch with a paper bag – this collects the flowers as they dry and fall from the stem. Hang the paper bag in a cool, dry place that has good air circulation. A dry verandah or pantry cupboard is perfect.

step four It will take six to eight weeks for the flowers to dry, depending on the weather conditions. It takes longer if the weather is humid.

step five The sachets can be made from muslin, calico, hessian or any other open weave fabric that will allow the aroma of the lavender flowers to escape. They can be stitched with thread or tied in bundles with string or coloured ribbons.

Lavender sachets are easy to make, and they are a great way to make the most of this sweetly fragrant and easy-to-grow plant.

step six The sachets make lovely gifts, and can be placed in clothing drawers and cupboards where the fragrance of the lavender will remain for more than a year.

the salad bowl

Grow your own salad vegetables in the summer and enjoy their wonderful fresh taste. A salad garden can be planted as part of a vegetable patch, or in containers on a sunny verandah or balcony.

tomatoes

Tomatoes are one of the most satisfying crops to grow because the flavour of the freshly picked fruits is so much more delicious than those bought from the supermarket. The larger varieties will need stakes to support them, while there are also smaller cherry or patio tomatoes that are ideal for containers.

growing tomatoes

Tomatoes must have lots of sun and warmth to produce fruits, so choose a position that has at least 6 hours of sun a day. The soil should be well drained and needs plenty of organic matter because tomato plants require plenty of nutrients. Avoid using poultry manure, as it will produce lots of foliage instead of lots of tomatoes. Large growing varieties will need to be tied to a stake to support the main growing stem, and this keeps the fruit up off the ground. The plants can get fungal problems, so always water at ground level (don't spray the leaves with water) and pick off any leaves that become spotted or mildewy. In hot, dry weather the tomato plants should be watered every day, to keep the fruits growing. As the plants begin to flower, apply some specially formulated tomato fertiliser (granular or liquid) to get a large crop of delicious fruits.

using tomatoes

Tomatoes are one of the most popular and versatile fruits – they can be used fresh in salads or cooked in sauces, casseroles or simply grilled as a wonderful and vitamin-rich side dish. Look for recipes on page 60.

did you know?

There are more than 7,000 different varieties of tomato around the world, and every year about 130 million tonnes of tomatoes are grown commercially. Tomatoes are more juicy and tasty if allowed to ripen while still on the plant. They can also be picked while still slightly green and ripened on a sunny windowsill.

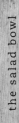

Tomatoes take several months to grow, depending on the variety. The cherry tomatoes grow more quickly, so plant seedlings in early spring so that you can enjoy harvesting juicy, red fruits by the middle of the summer.

tomatoes

During very hot summer weather protect the fruits from sunburn by tying an open umbrella to the garden stake during the hottest part of the day.

step one Buy seedlings rather than growing from seed as it's faster. Separate the seedlings, taking care not to damage the delicate root systems.

step two Fill a large terracotta pot with good quality potting mix. You can also incorporate some specially formulated tomato food to help the plants get off to a good start.

step three Hammer a stake into the centre of the pot. This will be used to support the tomato plant as it grows.

step four Plant the seedling next to the stake, making sure not to pile potting mix up around the base of the stem. Tie the plant loosely to the stake.

step five Water the seedling regularly as it grows, and keep tying the stem further up the stake to prevent it from collapsing.

step six When the flowers first appear apply some liquid fertiliser such as seaweed or fish emulsion.

The large tomato varieties will take 3-4 months for the fruit to ripen. The small cherry tomatoes ripen in just 2 months and will continue producing delicious fruits for 6 weeks.

tomato

Tomatoes have the best flavour when eaten warm, just after being picked. If you have a large crop, make tomato sauce for serving with pasta.

simple tomato sauce

4kg (8 pounds) ripe tomatoes
⅓ cup (80ml) olive oil
4 small brown onions (320g), chopped finely
8 cloves garlic, crushed
⅔ cup finely chopped fresh basil

1 Use a small knife to cut a small cross (not too deep) in the bottom of each tomato. Bring a large saucepan of water to the boil. Use tongs to carefully lower a few of the tomatoes into the boiling water. Leave them for about 10 seconds or until the skins just start to come away from the tomatoes. Take the tomatoes from the pan and put them in a large bowl filled with iced water. When they are cool enough to touch, peel off the skins. Keep doing this until all the tomatoes are peeled.
2 Cut the tomatoes in half; use a teaspoon to scoop out the seeds and throw them away. Chop the tomato flesh into chunks.
3 Heat the oil in a large saucepan, add the onion; cover the pan with a lid and cook, over low heat, 20 minutes, stirring the onion every now and then with a wooden spoon.
4 Add the garlic to the pan; cook, stirring, 5 minutes. Add the tomato flesh; cook, stirring, until tomato softens. Bring to the boil. Turn down the heat to low; simmer, uncovered, stirring every now and then, about 1½ hours or until mixture is the consistency of pasta sauce. Add the basil; cook, stirring, 10 minutes. Season to taste.
5 Pour the sauce into plastic freezer containers leaving 1-2cm (½-1 inch) space above the sauce for expansion. Cover, cool in refrigerator, then freeze for up to 6 months or store in the refrigerator for up to 5 days.
prep + cook time 2 hours 45 minutes
makes about 7 cups
nutritional count per 1 cup 10.8g total fat (1.5g saturated fat); 614kJ (147 cal); 7.2g carbohydrate; 3.2g protein; 4g fibre

roasted mixed tomato salad

4 small red tomatoes (360g), cut in half
4 small green tomatoes (360g), cut in half
250g (8 ounces) cherry tomatoes
200g (6½ ounces) red teardrop tomatoes
200g (6½ ounces) yellow teardrop tomatoes
2 tablespoons olive oil
2 tablespoons balsamic vinegar
2 tablespoons small fresh basil leaves
1 tablespoon each fresh oregano leaves and
    thyme leaves

1 Preheat oven to 240°C/475°F.
2 Put all the tomatoes and oil in a large shallow baking dish; mix well. Put the dish in the oven and roast 10 minutes. Wearing oven mitts, remove the dish from the oven; cool 30 minutes.
3 Put the tomato mixture and the rest of the ingredients in a large bowl, season to taste; mix well. Serve with grissini (breadsticks), if you like.
prep + cook time 20 minutes (+ cooling)
serves 10
nutritional count per serving 3.8g total fat (0.5g saturated fat); 209kJ (50 cal); 2.4g carbohydrate; 1g protein; 1.6g fibre

salad greens

No longer is lettuce the only green vegetable used to make a salad –
these days we love to add all sorts of colourful leaves of different
shapes and sizes. Some salad greens are fresh and sweet, and some
have a more peppery or bitter taste. Choose the ones you like
the best and create your own garden salad bowl.

about salad greens

There are dozens of different leafy green plants
that can be picked and used to make a fresh
and nutritious garden salad. Among the most
popular are lettuces, including the traditional
iceberg (round) lettuce, also red and green
mignonette and the popular cos (romaine)
lettuce, which also has red and green varieties.
Other salad greens include rocket, mustard
greens, baby spinach, chickory, endive, cress
and even flowering plants like nasturtium
and dandelions can be used in a salad.
Freshly sprouted alfalfa seeds are a great
salad addition.

growing salad greens

The secret to growing tasty salad greens is to
keep them growing rapidly, so that they can
be harvested while they are young and sweet
in flavour. Greens that have not been watered
regularly will slow down and taste bitter when
they are harvested. You can buy mixed punnets
of salad green seedlings or seed packets that
contain a range of different leaf varieties.

The soil should be quite rich, with organic
matter added, and plenty of sunshine will be
needed – at least 6 hours a day. A large, shallow
container can be used for growing greens,
and this could be placed in the sun near the
kitchen door for fast and easy harvesting.

using salad greens

Many salad greens can be harvested leaf by
leaf rather than picking the entire plant. Keep
picking the young leaves while they are fresh
and tender, wash them in cold water and
dry them in a salad spinner. The leaves can
be enjoyed for their own special flavour, or
sprinkled with a delicious dressing of olive oil
and lemon juice.

did you know?

Lettuce was originally cultivated by the
Egyptians around 450 BC and it was believed to
have 'soporific' qualities – which simply means
that people felt like going to sleep after eating
a big bowl of salad.

In warm climates salad
greens can be grown
all year around; in cool
regions they should be
planted from early spring
through to mid summer.

salad greens

step two Finely scatter the tiny seeds of three or four different small growing lettuce varieties such as green and red mignonette and baby cos. Cover the seeds with 1cm (½ inch) of potting mix and pat down lightly by hand.

step one Fill a large, shallow container with a good potting mixture that has a cupful of poultry pellets mixed into it. This is good for growing healthy foliage. The container must have drainage holes.

step three Use a fine water spray on the soil surface to prevent dislodging the seeds. The soil will need to be kept lightly moist for 2 weeks until the seedlings start to appear.

salad greens

5

step five Every 2 weeks
the lettuce will benefit
from a watering of liquid
organic fertiliser. They
will need to be grown in
a very sunny position to
get the best results.

4

step four Thin out the seedlings
if they are overcrowded. Allow
enough space around each
plant for it grow, following the
directions on the seed packet.

6

step six Harvest the lettuce
one at a time when they are fully
grown, or simply pick the leaves
as needed, leaving the plant in
the pot to continue growing and
producing more juicy foliage.

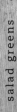

salad greens

rocket

This fast growing salad green is commonly called rocket because it takes off at speed, and can be harvested within a few weeks of first sowing seeds in the ground. It has a fresh, peppery taste and lots of vitamin C.

about rocket

Rocket is a member of the Brassica group, which means it is related to other edible plants such as cabbage, cauliflower and broccoli. It's a small growing annual plant that originally grew wild in Europe and is used extensively as a salad vegetable in many parts of the world.

growing rocket

Rocket is easy to grow because it germinates quickly from seed and seems to double in size overnight, producing bright green leaves that can be picked as you need them. Grow rocket in a sunny part of the herb garden or in a container positioned to get at least 5 hours of sun a day. Water the plants daily in summer to keep them growing quickly and plant fresh seeds every six weeks to keep a constant supply coming right through the summer.

using rocket

Rocket is best mixed with more bland salad leaves such as lettuce because it has a very strong flavour. It can also be cooked, like spinach or used as a garnish by chopping it finely and sprinkling it on soups or casseroles. Adding a few rocket leaves to a sandwich will give it some extra zip.

did you know?

In Italy there is an alcohol that is distilled from the leaves of the rocket plant. Called Rucolino, it is drunk at the end of the meal because it is believed to help with digestion.

You can grow rocket all year round as long as it's in a warm, sheltered position. Pick a few rocket leaves every time you make a fresh salad. The leaves will need to be washed and dried before being eaten.

cucumber

Fresh, crunchy cucumber is a terrific salad vegetable that
is easy to grow at home, either in the vegetable garden
or in a large container on a sunny balcony.

about cucumber

Cucumbers are members of the gourd family,
which are a group of vine-like plants that are
annuals and therefore need to be replanted
every springtime. It is believed cucumbers were
first cultivated in India about 3,000 years ago
and there are dozens of different varieties
including the very long, thin dark green
European varieties and a round white variety
that is commonly known as an apple cucumber.

growing cucumbers

Like a lot of vegetables, cucumbers need
good soil, lots of sunlight and plenty of water
during the summer growing period. They are a
creeping, annual vine so they also need some
sort of trellis or frame to climb on. This helps
to keep the developing fruits from lying on
the ground. Cucumbers are usually grown
from seed planted in spring and a healthy
plant will keep producing more fruits until
late in the season.

using cucumbers

Cucumbers are generally sliced and eaten raw
as part of a salad. Some people find cucumbers
make them burp a lot, and there are 'burpless'
varieties that seem to overcome this problem.
The skin of cucumber is quite tough and it can
be removed to make a more delicate salad.
There is a small cultivar of cucumber that can
be pickled – these are commonly called gherkins.

did you know?

Cucumbers need to be pollinated to produce
the flowers that will develop into the edible
fruits. So a healthy garden environment with
lots of bees buzzing around will ensure success.

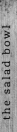

the salad bowl

Cucumbers are a summer crop that needs to be planted in early spring. You can plant a second crop in summer if you live in a warm climate. Pick cucumbers before they grow too large, as they will become tough and bitter if left on the vine for too long.

ladybird

butterfly

bird

spider

frog

dragonfly

bees

good creatures

There are many creatures, such as birds and various insects that help to make your garden a healthy environment for growing flowers, vegetables, herbs and fruit. These friendly beneficial helpers should be protected from predators, and always encouraged to come into the garden.

earthworm

centipede

fruit fly

aphid

pumpkin beetle

slug

caterpillar

cabbage moths

bad creatures

Some creatures cause lots of damage in the garden, chewing holes in foliage, laying eggs that hatch into very hungry caterpillars or small insects that suck sap from delicate flower buds. These creatures should be discouraged – not by spraying chemicals but by being hosed with a jet of water or by being trapped and removed.

snail

the magic garden

There are certain vegetables that can be easily grown in the garden without needing to buy seeds or seedlings from a nursery.

potatoes

Everybody loves potatoes. They are considered the most important of all vegetables and are widely grown as a food crop all around the world. There are hundreds of different varieties and although they require a bit of space in the garden, it's worth growing just a few plants because they taste so delicious when freshly dug from the ground.

about potatoes

Potatoes are in the same family as tomatoes, capsicum and peppers, however it's the tuberous root that is the valued, edible part of the plant. Potatoes were originally from north and south America, and they were taken to Europe in the 17th century where they became one of the most important agricultural crops.

growing potatoes

Potatoes are very easy to grow, multiplying under the ground during spring and summer. They are grown from tubers that have produced sprouts – often you will see potatoes in your kitchen vegetable bin with odd looking sprouts – these are the beginnings of a new plant. Commercial growers only use 'disease-free' tubers, however in the home garden you can just use old potatoes that have sprouted. They grow in any good garden soil. Dig a trench 25cm (10 inches) deep to plant the tubers, then cover with soil and water until the green foliage appears. The secret is to keep mounding soil up around the foliage, to make sure that the potatoes don't poke out of the ground as they are growing. It's amazing to harvest potatoes, because as you dig (carefully, so as not to stick a fork through any) you will uncover dozens of lovely new potatoes.

* Allow 25cm (10 inches) between each tuber that you plant.

using potatoes

Potatoes can be steamed in their skins, and this is the best way to maintain the vitamin content. They can be peeled, boiled and mashed or made into french fries. They are also wonderful in soup and stews – in fact they are a staple part of our diet and we should try and eat potatoes several times every week.

did you know?

When potatoes are exposed to light they turn green, and this makes them inedible because the flesh contains alkaloids, which are toxic. This is a natural protection mechanism, developed by the potato to protect it from predators.

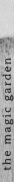

the magic garden

These magical plants provide us with their own seeds, sprouts or corms that can be planted in the garden where they will multiply and produce a fantastic crop.

creamy pumpkin & potato soup

1 tablespoon olive oil
1 medium brown onion (150g), chopped coarsely
1 clove garlic, crushed
600g (1¼ pounds) pumpkin, chopped coarsely
2 medium potatoes (400g), chopped coarsely
2 cups (500ml) water
1½ cups (375ml) vegetable stock
½ cup (125ml) pouring cream
1 tablespoon lemon juice
garlic and chive croûtons
⅓ loaf ciabatta (150g)
2 tablespoons olive oil
1 clove garlic, crushed
1 tablespoon finely chopped fresh chives

1 Heat the oil in a large saucepan; cook the onion and garlic, stirring with a wooden spoon, until onion softens. Add the pumpkin, potato, the water and stock; bring to the boil. Turn down the heat to low; put a lid on the pan and simmer the soup about 20 minutes or until vegetables are tender. Turn off the heat and leave the soup to cool for 15 minutes.
2 Meanwhile, make garlic and chive croûtons.
3 Blend or process soup, a little at a time, until smooth. Pour the blended soup back into the same cleaned pan; add the cream and juice. Reheat the soup, stirring, without boiling, until hot.
4 Serve bowls of soup topped with croûtons.
garlic and chive croûtons Preheat the oven to 180°C/350°F. Use a serrated bread knife to cut the bread into 2cm (¾-inch) cubes. Put the bread, oil, garlic and chives in a large bowl; mix well. Spread the bread onto an oven tray; put the tray in the oven and toast the bread until browned.
prep + cook time 35 minutes **serves** 4
nutritional count per serving 29.3g total fat (11.7g saturated fat); 2006kJ (480 cal); 41.4g carbohydrate; 10.7g protein; 5g fibre

TIP In Italian, the word "ciabatta" means slipper, the traditional shape of this popular crisp-crusted, open-textured white sourdough bread. It is a good bread to use for bruschetta.

corn-filled potatoes

8 potatoes (960g), unpeeled
1 teaspoon vegetable oil
30g (1 ounce) sliced prosciutto, chopped
125g (4 ounces) canned creamed corn
2 tablespoons finely chopped fresh
  coriander (cilantro)

1 Preheat oven to 200°C/400°F. Oil an oven tray.
2 Boil, steam or microwave whole potatoes until just tender; drain. Leave to cool.
3 Meanwhile, heat oil in a small frying pan; cook prosciutto, stirring, about 2 minutes or until crisp. Remove prosciutto from the pan with a slotted spoon; drain on absorbent paper.
4 Cut a shallow slice from top of each potato; use a teaspoon to scoop the flesh from tops into a medium bowl, discard skin. Scoop about two-thirds of the flesh from each potato into the same bowl; reserve the potato shells.
5 Mash potato flesh until smooth; stir in corn, prosciutto and coriander. Season. Place potato shells on tray; spoon potato mixture into shells. Bake 15 minutes or until heated through.
prep + cook time 45 minutes **serves** 4
nutritional count per serving 2g total fat (0.3g saturated fat); 878kJ (210 cal); 36.7g carbohydrate; 7.8g protein; 5.9g fibre

pumpkins

Save the seeds from inside a pumpkin and germinate them to produce new plants from old. You will need to collect the seeds of fully ripe pumpkins and store them for sowing in the ground the following spring.

about pumpkins

Pumpkins are in the Curcubit family and related to cucumbers and zucchini. All these plants originally came from north and south America but they are now grown worldwide and enjoyed in many of our favourite recipes. There are dozens of different varieties, from small the orange 'Golden Nugget' to the large 'Queensland Blue'.

how to grow pumpkins

Cut open a ripe pumpkin and scoop out the pulp and seeds from inside. Carefully separate the seeds from the pulp and wash the seeds in cold water, holding them in a colander. Now spread the seeds out on a sheet of newspaper and allow them to completely dry – in a shaded but well ventilated area. When dried the seeds can be stored in a paper bag to be planted the following spring.

Pumpkins need a long, hot summer and quite rich soil to grow well. Make a mound of soil and then form a dish-like hole in the centre. Simply plant two or three seeds in the hole, cover with soil and water until the seedlings appear. Remove the weakest seedling and mulch around the plants with some well-rotted manure as these plants are greedy for nutrients. Take care to water the remaining ones every day during summer as they need lots of moisture to keep growing vigorously. Wait until all the foliage and stems have died back in autumn before harvesting your delicious pumpkins.

* Plant seeds 3cm (1¼ inches) deep, allowing 45cm (18 inches) between planting mounds.

using pumpkins

Pumpkin can be baked in the oven, or steamed and mashed with lots of butter. In America pumpkin pie is also a popular recipe – it's a sweet pie served with whipped cream.

did you know?

Seeds are available for growing enormous pumpkins often entered into competitions at country agricultural shows. The world's largest pumpkin was a variety called 'Atlantic Giant' and weighed 782.45 kilograms.

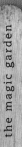

Make sure the ground around the pumpkins is mulched with straw. This will stop the skin of the pumpkin from sitting directly on the soil which can cause it to rot.

garlic

Garlic is easy to grow, although it takes about eight months from the time you plant the cloves until the time you can dig up the mature bulbs. They are worth waiting for.

about garlic

Garlic is a member of the onion family, known as Alliums, and related to red, brown and white onions, shallots and also leeks. Originally found growing wild all across Europe, garlic has been adopted by almost every country as one of the world's favourite plants for flavouring food. It grows as an underground bulb and produces tall, slender stems and circular flower heads

growing garlic

In mild climates garlic can be grown all year round, however in cooler regions you will need to plant the bulbs in spring for harvesting in summer. Buy locally grown garlic and allow it to sit in a dark, dry place for a couple of weeks, until the individual cloves start to produce tiny green and white shoots. Carefully separate the cloves and plant them with the shoot side upwards in a well dug-over area of the garden. The soil should have some well rotted manure dug in and the cloves need to be about 8cm (3 inches) apart. Water them two or three times a week if the weather is dry. When the

flowers have finished and the foliage starts to turn brown and die back, it's time to dig up your new bulbs – each little clove will have developed into a full size garlic bulb.
* *Plant the cloves at a depth of 4cm (1½ inches), and allow 10cm (4 inches) between plantings.*

using garlic

Garlic is sliced or crushed and added to soups, stews and salad dressings. It has a very powerful flavour and should be used sparingly until you are entirely used to it. There is a delicious mayonnaise using lots of garlic, known as aïoli, and it is wonderful served with seafood, especially prawns.

did you know?

As garlic has such a strong smell, even when it's growing in the ground, it is a useful plant to repel insects that attack other plants in the garden. It's great to grow next to tomato plants. In ancient times garlic was believed to ward off evil spirits and vampires, and a necklace of garlic was sometimes worn by people who thought it would protect them.

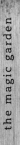

This is baby garlic, picked before it has matured. At this stage it has a mild taste.

painted pots

Painting and decorating pots are environmentally-friendly and inexpensive ways to make your garden look amazing. These fun craft projects use everyday objects and make ideal gifts.

newspaper creations

Wrap newspaper around a can to form the pot shape. Fold newspaper underneath the can to form a base and hold in place with sticky tape. Remove the can. Decorate the paper with strips and shapes of cardboard and ribbons. Fill the paper pot with soil and add a seedling or a cutting. You can plant it directly into the soil as the newspaper will decompose.

egg people Paint faces on the front of egg cartons to look like each person in your family. Fill each hole with a little soil, sprinkle some seeds then a little more soil to cover. Alfalfa seeds will grow quickly and look like hair (see also page 12). You can plant any seeds in egg cartons. If the carton is biodegradable, once the seeds become seedlings you can plant them directly into the ground – carton and all.

hessian sacks Wrap a piece of hessian around an empty, cleaned can to form the pot shape, then cut out the fabric using the can's width as a guide. Sew the short ends together. Using the base of the can as a guide, cut out a circle leaving a 1cm (½ inch) border; stitch the circle into the base of the hessian pot. Make a few holes in the base of the can for drainage, reinsert into the hessian pot then add soil and seeds or a seedling. You could also pot plants directly into the hessian pot, then directly into the ground.

potato stamp pots To make the potato stamp, cut a potato in half then press a shaped cookie cutter into the cut side. Using a knife, cut about 5mm (¼ inch) off the top of the potato around the shape to make it look 3D. Using a paintbrush apply the paint onto the cut out shape. Gently press the shape onto the pot. Create any design you want by making a few stamps with different shapes and colours.

painted cans This is a fun and easy way to recycle tin cans. Wash the empty cans with warm soapy water, then rinse and dry well. Make a few holes in the base of each can for drainage. Using paintbrushes and acrylic paint, create your own colourful designs and patterns. Finish off with a top coat of varnish.

chalk pots Use any container you like (a box or can) but make sure you make holes in the base for drainage. Apply a few coats of blackboard paint to the outside surface, letting it dry for about 5 hours after each coat. When you've finished painting, leave the container for a day so the paint can dry completely. Using coloured chalk create your own designs: draw worms, roots or write the name of the potted plants.

painted pots

mushroom kits

Mushrooms are not a vegetable but a fungus. There are lots of varieties that grow in the wild, many of them are poisonous so never try eating them unless an expert has positively identified them as being edible.

step three Spray the soil surface with a mist of water to make it damp. This will provide exactly the right growing conditions for the mushrooms.

step one Mushroom growing kits are available at most garden shops and nurseries, and they contain all the necessary components to produce a healthy crop of fresh mushrooms.

step two Carefully fill the plastic-lined box with the soil mix, which will have already been sown with mycelium (the spores that produce the mushroom fungus). Follow the directions that come with the kit.

The compost in which your mushrooms have grown is an excellent soil builder in the garden. After all the mushrooms have been harvested, simply add it to your compost heap.

step four Take the kit into a dark, well ventilated place. A dark airy cupboard or a cellar under the house are perfect places for keeping the kits while the mushrooms grow.

step five Check the kit every few days, and spray with more water if the soil mix has started to dry out. Depending on the temperature, tiny white spots will start appearing after a week or so. These are the beginning of the mushrooms.

step six Harvest the mushrooms when they reach the size recommended according to the kit's directions. This will change depending on the variety. Yum!

mushroom & spinach tarts with tomato salad

150g (4½ ounces) baby spinach leaves
20g (¾ ounce) butter
300g (9½ ounces) button mushrooms, sliced thinly
1 egg, beaten lightly
250g (8 ounces) ricotta cheese
2 tablespoons finely shredded fresh basil
2 sheets puff pastry, cut in half
tomato salad
2 tablespoons pine nuts, roasted
250g (8 ounces) grape tomatoes, cut in half
2 small vine-ripened tomatoes (180g), sliced thickly
1 tablespoon olive oil
1 tablespoon lemon juice
½ cup loosely packed fresh basil leaves

1 Preheat oven to 220°C/425°F. Line two oven trays with baking paper.
2 Keep 1 cup of loosely packed spinach leaves to use later. Melt the butter in a large frying pan over high heat; cook mushrooms, stirring with a wooden spoon, until browned and tender. Add the rest of the spinach; cook, stirring, until spinach begins to wilt. Remove mushroom mixture from pan with a slotted spoon; drain the mixture on absorbent paper.
3 Put the egg, cheese and shredded basil in a medium bowl, season; mix well.
4 Place the pastry rectangles on the prepared trays. Spread the cheese mixture evenly over pastry rectangles, leaving a 1.5cm (¾-inch) border; fold the borders in and press down firmly. Top with the mushroom mixture.
5 Put the trays in the oven and bake about 20 minutes or until pastry is browned and crisp.
6 Meanwhile, make tomato salad.
7 Serve tarts topped with the reserved cup of spinach leaves; serve tarts with the tomato salad.
tomato salad Put all the ingredients in a large bowl, season to taste; mix well.
prep + cook time 40 minutes **serves** 4
nutritional count per serving 41.5g total fat (18.7g saturated fat); 2495kJ (597 cal); 34.9g carbohydrate; 18.4g protein; 6.1g fibre

Chickens not only provide us with fresh eggs, they produce nitrogen-rich manure to add to the compost heap.

the cactus garden

Cactus and succulents are plants that have swollen stems and roots, which allows them to store water for long periods. This is why they only need to be watered when the soil in the pot has completely dried out.

step two Handle the cactus with great care. You will need gloves and some squares of paper towel because the sharp spines make the cactus very difficult to handle.

step one Fill a shallow terracotta pot with a soil mix that has been specifically designed for growing cactus. It must be light and well drained, and drainage holes in the base of the pot are essential.

step three Using the paper towel to support the plant, position it in the container, taking care not to disturb the delicate root system. Press down lightly around the plant once it has been positioned.

step five Cover the soil surface with fine gravel. This helps to recreate the environment where cactus are naturally found growing – and it looks great as well.

step four Choose a variety of different shaped plants to achieve a more interesting effect. You can mix cactus and succulents together to create a really fascinating garden.

step six Put your cactus garden in the sunniest place you can find and water the pot no more than once a week. Overwatering is the most common mistake made when growing cactus.

Cactus can be grown
outside in the garden,
but they are also great
houseplants and should
be placed on a sunny
windowsill, which
will provide a perfect
environment for flowering.

the vegie garden

The best fun you can have in the garden is planting your own vegetables, watching them grow and then harvesting them. Vegetable gardens need lots of sun and good soil.

beetroot

onion

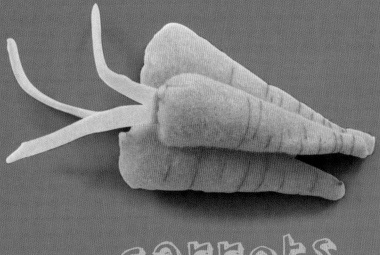

carrots

Nothing is more crunchy and delicious than a homegrown carrot freshly pulled up from the vegie garden and rinsed under a tap, and then eaten on-the-spot. Carrots are mysterious because while they are growing all you see above ground are the bright green leafy tops, meanwhile underneath the ground those bright orange roots should be growing vigorously.

about carrots

Carrots are related to parsnips, celery and parsley, all of which were originally wild plants in Europe that were first cultivated by the Romans more than a thousand years ago. They are grown as annual plants, which means that the seeds are generally sown in spring and the carrots harvested in autumn – if left in the ground they will continue to grow through the winter and then flower the following spring.

growing carrots

Carrots are quite fiddly plants to grow because the seed is so tiny that it gets tricky to sow them without having too many plants close together. You need to prepare the ground well, digging quite deeply, so that the carrots can send their long orange roots (that we love to eat) down into the ground. Then sprinkle the tiny seeds in straight rows and cover with a fine layer of soil. Keep this watered with a fine spray every day until the little green tops appear. When these are about 6cm (2½ inches)

high you will need to thin them by pulling up quite a few of the tiny plants so that the ones remaining have enough space to grow properly. Try and keep the weeds from growing around the carrots, and just keep watering a few times a week until autumn, when you can start pulling up your carrots.

using carrots

Carrots are rich in vitamins and are delicious eaten raw in salads, or grated and made into a French-style entrée with raisins and an olive-oil dressing. Carrots are also used in soups and casseroles because they add sweetness and colour.

did you know?

We always think of carrots as being orange, but there are purple, white, red and yellow varieties available in some countries. Carrots are often grown as companion plants in rows next to tomatoes, because they mysteriously improve the tomato crop.

Pick every third small sweet carrot along the row – this will give space for those remaining in the ground to grow larger. The green carrot tops can be cut off and used in the compost, or fed to your chickens.

spicy carrot & pineapple muffins

⅓ cup (50g) plain (all-purpose) flour
½ cup (75g) self-raising flour
½ teaspoon bicarbonate of soda (baking soda)
¼ cup (55g) caster (superfine) sugar
½ teaspoon ground cinnamon
225g (7 ounces) canned crushed pineapple, drained well
⅔ cup (160g) firmly packed finely grated carrot
⅓ cup (80ml) vegetable oil
1 egg, beaten lightly

1 Preheat oven to 180°C/350°F. Grease 6-hole (⅓ cup/80ml) standard muffin pan.
2 Put the flours, soda, sugar and cinnamon into a flour sifter or sieve and sift into a medium bowl. Add the pineapple, carrot, oil and egg to bowl; stir with a wooden spoon until the ingredients come together (do not over-mix). Spoon the mixture equally into muffin pan holes.
3 Put the pan in the oven and bake for about 20 minutes. Wearing your oven mitts, take the pan out of the oven and leave the cakes in pan for 5 minutes before turning them onto a wire rack to cool.
prep + cook time 30 minutes **makes** 6
nutritional count per muffin 13.4g total fat (1.9g saturated fat); 903kJ (216 cal); 28.6g carbohydrate; 3.7g protein; 2.1g fibre

TIP This recipe will also make 24 mini muffins. Use two greased 12-hole (1-tablespoon/20ml) mini muffin pans and cook them for about 15 minutes.

spinach & eggplant lasagne stacks

1 tablespoon olive oil
2 stalks celery (300g), trimmed, chopped finely
1 medium brown onion (150g), chopped finely
2 cloves garlic, crushed
500g (1 pound) minced (ground) beef
2⅔ cups (700g) bottled tomato pasta sauce
2 tablespoons tomato paste
¼ cup finely chopped fresh flat-leaf parsley
2 medium eggplants (600g)
60g (2 ounces) baby spinach leaves
1 cup (120g) coarsely grated cheddar cheese
cheese sauce
40g (1½ ounces) butter
2 tablespoons plain (all-purpose) flour
1½ cups (375ml) milk, warmed
½ cup (60g) coarsely grated cheddar cheese

1 Heat the oil in a large saucepan; cook celery, onion and garlic, stirring, until onion softens. Add the beef; cook, stirring and breaking up any large lumps with the back of the spoon, until the meat changes colour. Add the sauce and paste; bring to the boil. Turn down the heat to low and simmer, uncovered, about 20 minutes or until the sauce becomes thick. Stir in the parsley; season to taste.
2 Meanwhile, make cheese sauce.
3 Cut the eggplant into 18 long, thin slices. Cook the slices, a few at a time, on a heated oiled grill plate (or grill or barbecue) until browned lightly and tender. Preheat grill (broiler).
4 Evenly stack three layers of meat sauce, spinach leaves, eggplant slices and cheese sauce on each of six heatproof serving plates. Sprinkle with cheese. Put each plate under the grill until cheese melts.
cheese sauce Melt butter in a medium saucepan, add flour; cook, stirring, about 1 minute or until the mixture bubbles and thickens. Add the milk, a little at a time, stirring until smooth before adding more milk; keep doing this until all the milk is added. Cook, stirring, until the sauce boils and thickens. Turn off the heat; stir the cheese into the sauce.
prep + cook time 1 hour 10 minutes **serves** 6
nutritional count per serving 29.2g total fat (14.5g saturated fat); 1994kJ (477 cal); 20.1g carbohydrate; 31.1g protein; 7g fibre

carrot dip

5 medium carrots (600g), chopped coarsely
1 tablespoon olive oil
1 clove garlic, crushed
½ teaspoon ground cumin
2 teaspoons lemon juice
⅓ cup (95g) yogurt

1 Boil, steam or microwave the carrot until tender; drain.
2 Heat the oil in a large frying pan; cook the garlic and cumin, stirring with a wooden spoon, about 1 minute or until you can smell the spices. Stir in the carrot and juice. Turn off the heat; leave the carrot mixture to cool for 10 minutes.
3 Put the carrot mixture and yogurt in a blender or food processor; blend or process until the dip is smooth. Season to taste. Serve dip with grissini (breadsticks), if you like.
prep + cook time 40 minutes **serves** 6
nutritional count per serving 3.5g total fat (0.7g saturated fat); 276kJ (66 cal); 5.7g carbohydrate; 1.7g protein; 2.6g fibre

Baby spinach is sweet and crunchy when eaten raw in salads or as part of a pasta recipe.

spinach

Spinach is a fast growing crop with deep green leaves that are very rich in vitamins and packed with flavour. There are several varieties, and the easiest for the home gardener are the 'baby spinach' types.

about spinach

Spinach is a cool climate foliage plant originally grown in the mountainous regions of Europe and Asia. It contains high levels of iron and vitamins, which is why it has always been highly valued as a culinary plant.

growing spinach

In most regions spinach can only be successfully grown in the cooler months of the year, because in summer it will produce flowering stems and seeds before the leaves have time to develop. You can buy punnets of 'baby spinach' which is a variety that can be grown very quickly in rich moist soil, and harvested when the leaves are still very small and tender. You will need several plants to produce sufficient leaves and you can harvest them while leaving the plant growing – hopefully it will produce a second or third batch of leaves for harvesting. Baby spinach is best grown in autumn and winter as the plants bolt to seed during hot summer weather.
• Silver beet is also sometimes called spinach, and it is a much easier plant to grow in most climates. The leaves are tougher, but one or two plants will provide enough for an average family right through the summer. Plant seeds of silver beet in spring and water well.
• Silver beet is also called swiss chard and there are varieties with brilliant red, orange and yellow stems that look really beautiful growing in the garden – almost too pretty to harvest and eat.
* Plant seeds at a depth of 1cm (½ inch) and allow a distance of 15cm (6 inches) between spinach plants and 30cm (12 inches) between silver beet plants.

using spinach

Spinach leaves can be used raw in a salad of mixed greens, or steamed lightly and eaten as a vegetable side dish. It can also be used in Asian stir-fries, or chopped and added to soup.

did you know?

One of the Queens of France, Catherine de Medici, loved spinach so much she ordered it to be served at every meal. The cartoon character Popeye ate canned spinach to give him magical strength.

the vegie garden

Pick spinach leaves
every few days, and
more leaves will
grow to replace them.
Water the plants
regularly to maintain
healthy growth.

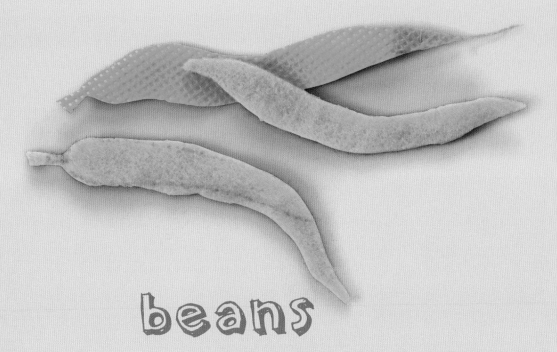

beans

Beans are easy to grow and you can plant either climbing or bush varieties, depending on how much space you have in the garden. They are rich in vitamins and taste ten times better when picked and eaten on the same day.

about beans

Sometimes called french beans, these useful plants are legumes and related to more than a hundred different edible plants including all the dried beans varieties that we use in soups and popular foods like baked beans. For the gardener there are lots of choices, including green, purple and 'butter bean' varieties.

growing beans

Beans are best grown from seed planted directly in the ground. The soil for beans needs to be quite rich in organic matter, and it's a good idea to dig a little dolomite lime into the ground a couple of weeks before sowing the seeds. If you are growing climbing beans you will need a trellis or a tripod of bamboo stakes so that the bean plants can wind around them as they grow. If you are growing bush beans simply plant them in a row, about 15cm (6 inches) apart. Beans need soil with lots of organic matter and regular watering once the seeds have germinated. You can start planting seed in spring and then plant a second crop in summer to continue harvesting well into autumn.

* Bean seeds should be planted at a depth of 3cm (1¼ inches), and allow 4-5cm (1½-2 inches) between plants.

using beans

Beans can be eaten raw, although most recipes call for them to be lightly steamed and used in salads or as a vegetable side dish. They are great in stir-fries or tossed in butter with crushed garlic to enhance their natural flavour. They are a vegetable that can be blanched in boiling water and frozen, which is great if there are too many beans produced at one time.

did you know?

Beans are best when picked young and tender, however if some of the beans have grown too large and tough they can be left on the vine where they will eventually dry out. Save these seeds in paper bag and plant them next spring.

radish & orange salad with popcorn

¼ cup (60ml) vegetable oil
40g (1½ ounces) butter
¼ cup (60g) popping corn
¼ teaspoon sea salt flakes
4 medium oranges (1kg)
1 cup (50g) snow pea sprouts
½ cup (125ml) pomegranate pulp
6 red radishes (210g), trimmed, sliced thinly
orange dressing
¼ cup (60ml) olive oil
2 tablespoons orange juice
1 tablespoon white wine vinegar
1 teaspoon honey

1 Heat the oil in a medium saucepan; add butter and popping corn. Put a lid on the pan; cook, over high heat, shaking the pan until corn stops popping. Turn off the heat; be careful the pan will be hot. Spoon the popcorn onto a tray lined with absorbent paper; drain well, then sprinkle with salt.
2 Make orange dressing.
3 Peel the oranges; cut the oranges into thin round slices.
4 Stack orange slices, sprouts, pomegranate and radish in serving bowls; drizzle with the dressing, sprinkle the popcorn on top.
orange dressing Put all of the ingredients in a screw-top jar; shake well.
prep + cook time 20 minutes **serves** 8
nutritional count per serving 18.2g total fat (4.6g saturated fat); 1003kJ (240 cal); 14.9g carbohydrate; 2.6g protein; 4.3g fibre

TIP You need to buy a medium pomegranate (320g) to get ½ cup pulp. To remove the pulp from the pomegranate, cut it in half, then hold the fruit, cut-side down, over a bowl and hit the back of the fruit with a wooden spoon – the seeds usually fall out easily. Discard the shell and white pith.

bean & potato salad

6 medium potatoes (650g), cut into four wedges
1 tablespoon olive oil
1 cup (180g) baby black olives, seeds removed
250g (8 ounces) green beans, trimmed, halved
thyme vinaigrette
¼ cup (60ml) olive oil
2 tablespoons white wine vinegar
1 clove garlic, crushed
2 teaspoons fresh lemon thyme leaves

1 Preheat oven to 200°C/400°F.
2 Whisk ingredients for thyme vinaigrette in a large bowl.
3 Combine potatoes and oil in a large baking dish. Roast in oven 1 hour or until the potatoes are tender. Wearing oven mitts, take the dish out of the oven. Using tongs, add hot potatoes and olives to the vinaigrette; mix well. Cool.
4 Meanwhile, boil, steam or microwave beans until tender; drain. Rinse under cold water; drain.
5 Stir beans into potato mixture; season.
prep + cook time 1 hour 15 minutes **serves** 8
nutritional count per serving 10g total fat (1.4g saturated fat); 711kJ (170 cal); 15.7g carbohydrate; 2.8g protein; 2.7g fibre

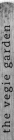

the vegie garden

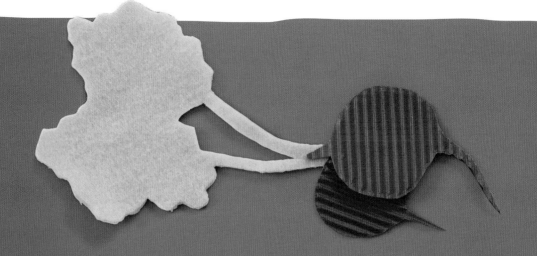

radishes

These crunchy little vegetables have a peppery flavour and they are great fun to grow because they are probably the fastest crop you will ever plant. They gallop from seed to harvest in just a couple of weeks.

about radishes

Radishes are related to other members of the Brassica family, including cabbage and broccoli, although you would never know it to look at them. They are called a 'root' vegetable because the swollen red and white root is the edible portion, and it grows half in and out of the ground making it easy to see the right time for harvesting. They are native to most of Europe and Asia and have been cultivated for more than 2,000 years. In European countries that are a minor salad crop, but in Asia they are an important root vegetable and there are dozens of different varieties.

growing radishes

These are very unfussy plants, and they should always be grown from seed planted directly in the ground. The seed is very small and you need to dig a shallow trench and sprinkle the seed as finely as possible then cover with soil and water in. Within a couple of days the first shoots will appear and you can thin out some if they appear overcrowded. Harvest every second or third radish along the row, allowing space for the rest to grow a little larger.

• *Plant seeds no more than 1cm (½ inch) deep, and allow about 3cm (1¼ inches) between plants.*

using radishes

Radish is generally eaten raw as a salad vegetable, although there are different, larger varieties that are an important part of Asian cuisine and are cooked in stir-fries and sometimes pickled or preserved as a gourmet treat.

did you know?

In Egyptian times radishes were popular and are believed to have been an important part of the rations fed to the thousands of labourers who helped build the Great Pyramids.
There is a variety called the rat-tailed radish, which produces long, thin seedpods that are eaten instead of the root.

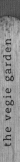

Plant radish seeds all year round in warm climates; only plant in spring and summer if you live in a cold region. You will be surprised by how quickly they grow. Crunchy radishes are delicious in salads, or they can be eaten on their own as a snack.

capsicum

Capsicums are also known as peppers and they are related to chillies and tomatoes, and have very similar growing requirements. They are a summer vegetable, planted in spring and harvested right through until autumn.

about capsicums

Vitamin-rich capsicums are native to Mexico and Central America, and they include a wide range of edible plants including sweet peppers and bell peppers, which are mild in flavour, and cayenne peppers, which are very hot and spicy. Although cultivated for thousands of years, capsicums and peppers were not introduced to western countries until 400 years ago.

growing capsicums

Capsicums can be grown from seed or from seedlings. Buying seedlings will give you a bit of a head start because they take a long time to produce mature fruits. Capsicums prefer soil that has had lots of well-rotted manure dug into it, and they need full sun – as many hours in the day as possible. It's a good idea to provide a stake to support the main stem of the plant as it grows. As the fruits get bigger the plant may topple over if not tied to a stake or trellis. Regular watering is also important,

as the fleshy fruits absorb a lot of moisture through the roots.

* Plant the seedlings at least 45cm (18 inches) apart.

using capsicums

Cooked or raw, capsicums have a delicious flavour that makes it one of our most popular vegetables. They are wonderful sliced into a salad or diced and used in soups and stews. They can also be grilled, to remove the skin, and then preserved in olive oil. In Poland and Hungary capsicums are dried and used to make a spice known as paprika.

did you know?

Capsicums (and chillies) are high in vitamin C and their peppery flavour can be used to make a liquid spray that will keep possums away from the garden. Simply mince a capsicum in a blender with water, strain into a spray bottle and apply around plants that possums love.

Spring is always the best planting time for capsicums. Capsicum are tasty eaten raw in salads, or cooked on the barbecue and drizzled with fragrant olive oil.

cauliflower gratin

6 baby cauliflowers (750g), trimmed
50g (1½ ounces) butter
¼ cup (35g) plain (all-purpose) flour
1½ cups (375ml) milk, warmed
½ cup (60g) coarsely grated cheddar cheese
¼ cup (20g) finely grated parmesan cheese
1 tablespoon packaged breadcrumbs

1 Preheat oven to 220°C/425°F.
2 Boil, steam or microwave the cauliflowers until tender; drain. Put cauliflowers in a medium shallow ovenproof dish.
3 Meanwhile, melt the butter in a medium saucepan, add the flour; cook, stirring with a wooden spoon or whisk, about 1 minute or until the mixture bubbles and thickens. Add the milk, a little at a time, stirring until smooth before adding more milk; keep doing this until all the milk is added. Cook, stirring, until the sauce boils and thickens. Turn off the heat; stir the cheeses into the sauce. Season to taste.
4 Pour the cheese sauce over cauliflower in dish; sprinkle with the breadcrumbs. Put the dish in the oven and bake about 15 minutes or until the top is browned lightly.
prep + cook time 30 minutes **serves** 6
nutritional count per serving 14.1g total fat (9g saturated fat); 865kJ (207 cal); 10.2g carbohydrate; 9.1g protein; 2.2g fibre

capsicum hummus

1 small red capsicum (bell pepper) (150g)
400g (12½ ounces) canned chickpeas
   (garbanzo beans), rinsed, liquid drained
¼ cup (60ml) water
¼ cup (70g) tahini
2 tablespoons lemon juice
2 tablespoons olive oil
1 clove garlic, crushed

1 Preheat oven to 220°C/425°F.
2 Put the capsicum on a baking-paper-lined oven tray. Put the tray in the oven and roast 30 minutes or until the capsicum is blistered and blackened. Wearing your oven mitts, take the tray out of the oven; cover the capsicum with plastic or paper and leave for 5 minutes. When capsicum is cool enough to touch, peel off the skin. Chop capsicum flesh into chunks.
3 Put capsicum and the rest of the ingredients in a blender or food processor; blend or process until hummus is smooth. Season. Serve with toasted wholemeal pitta triangles.
prep + cook time 40 minutes **serves** 6
nutritional count per serving 14.1g total fat (1.9g saturated fat); 769kJ (184 cal); 7.2g carbohydrate; 5.6g protein; 4g fibre

cauliflowers

Cauliflowers are slow growing plants that take up quite a bit of space in the garden but are worthwhile planting because of the wonderful, fresh flavour they have when home-grown.

about cauliflowers

Cauliflowers are annual plants that are related to cabbage, broccoli and Brussels sprouts. They are native plants of Europe, although there are also varieties that once grew wild in central Asia. They can take up to six months to mature, although there are now miniature varieties that will be ready for harvesting after only 12 weeks.

growing cauliflowers

Cauliflowers are hungry plants, which means they need good soil with lots of organic matter to provide them with enough nutrients to keep growing steadily. The main problem is if they are not watered often enough they will slow down and fail to produce lovely big white flower heads for harvesting. Water every day in summer, and use a liquid fertiliser to keep the cauliflowers growing steadily. The trick to keeping the head of the cauliflower white is

to tie the outside leaves together over the top, keeping the sun from turning the edible part of the plant yellow. Mulch around them with some manure and that should help keep the soil moist while feeding the plants at the same time.

using cauliflowers

Cauliflower can be cut up into individual florets, which can be dipped into a savoury sauce and eaten raw. They are also cooked and served with a delicious cheese sauce or simply steamed and served with butter and pepper.

did you know?

There are also orange, green and purple cauliflower varieties and there is also one called 'Romanesque' that looks like a miniature Christmas tree – green and pointed at the top.

In warm climates plant cauliflowers in late summer and autumn and they will keep growing through the winter. In colder regions you can plant all year, except mid winter.

Scarecrow

Scarecrows have traditionally been used to help keep certain birds such as crows and sparrows from coming into the garden and eating the seed or damaging the seedlings. Even if you don't have a bird problem, making a scarecrow is an exciting project and it will make the vegetable patch look like much more fun. Just not for the birds!

step three Cut a large square of hessian or heavy fabric such as upholstery material. Place over head and gather at base of neck and secure it with twine. Allow excess fabric to flare out from the neck. It can be trimmed later if need be.

step one Position two wooden stakes in the shape of a crucifix, the horizontal stake being slightly shorter than the vertical, the vertical one with the sharp end facing down. Tie twine around both stakes until it feels secure.

step two Roll some wadding into a ball shape and then wrap twine around the ball to keep its shape. Impale ball onto wooden stake (this is the head). If needed, wrap more twine around head then around join of the two stakes. This will stop the head from coming off.

scarecrow

step four Cut thick wadding into wide strips and wrap around top three-quarters of crucifix, including arms, to form a body. Wrap twine around until wadding stays in place then tie to secure. For the hands and waist cut the bristles of an old natural fibre broom (you can use straw or raffia if unavailable) and tie in bunches to ends of arms and where the wadding stops at waist.

step five Use an old shirt to dress the scarecrow (you can use a dress if you want a girl) and tie up the wrists and waist with twine. You can add a hat to his head and patches to his clothes if you like. Buttons or the bottom of tin cans with two holes nailed in them can be sewn on for eyes. Sew a simple smile on in running stitch out of thick cotton or wool.

step six Give your scarecrow a name then find a nice place for him to stand in your garden. Push the stake into soil until the scarecrow feels sturdy.

the strawberry patch

Strawberries like plenty of sunshine and the ground should be well prepared with organic matter, dug well into the soil before planting time. You may need to cover the plants with bird netting as the fruits start to ripen – they are very popular with many common garden birds.

step one Prepare a bed by removing all the weeds and digging the soil over lightly. Add some homemade compost or half a bag of well rotted cow manure and dig this in before planting.

step two Carefully remove the strawberry plants from their pots, taking care not to damage their roots. Plant them at least 25cm (10 inches) apart, and firm the soil down well around each plant.

step three Water in well, and keep watering every 3 or 4 days, especially if the weather is hot and dry. A liquid organic fertiliser should also be used every 4 weeks to help fruit production.

step four After watering well, mulch with a good layer of straw to prevent the soil from drying out too quickly. This also stops the strawberries from touching the ground and spoiling.

step five Pick the strawberries when they are fully ripe but still firm. They are best eaten on the same day that they have been picked.

step six If the strawberries have been kept off the ground and not attacked by slugs or snails, then they should not require washing before eating.

Set aside a separate area of the garden just for growing strawberries, which are perennial plants that should produce delicious bright red berries year after year.

daisy chain

There are many different types of daisy flowers, from these tiny English lawn daisies to larger pink and yellow flowering varieties. They all make pretty daisy chains.

the school garden

broadbeans

ROCKET

Leeks

SOY BEAN

The fun of school and community gardens is that you can get together with friends and work hard to create a really beautiful and healthy environment.

School gardens are a great way of helping kids to understand how fruit and vegetables are grown. This is particularly good for city children who may not have seen a vegetable garden or had the experience of picking fresh fruit.

Don't forget to wear a hat while working in the garden. It's also best to wear gardening gloves while you're handling soil.

the flower garden

It's possible to have flowers in the garden all year round if you choose a variety of shrubs, annuals and perennials that flower in different seasons. Look for flowers that are fragrant and colourful.

WAGON MASTER—60

paper daisies

frangipani

nasturtium

lisianthus

geranium

cyclamen

daisy

lavender

gum blossom

tulip

bougainvillea

pansy

freesia

flannel flowers

gerbera

snapdragon

hyacinth

rose

chrysanthemum

the flower garden

all about flowers

Flowers grow on trees and shrubby bushes; they cascade from vines and other climbing plants; they can be produced by bulbs and corms; by perennial ground covers; and they also grow as annuals, which means that you plant them from seeds or seedlings every spring or summer. Flowers don't just make the garden look pretty. They have a role to play in attracting birds and bees, and in helping to create an environmental balance, which is the ultimate aim of every keen gardener.

flowering house plants

If you don't have an outdoor garden, there are lots of pretty flowering plants that can be grown in pots, positioned on a sunny windowsill or in an area that has plenty of bright light. Look for cyclamen, begonias, African violets, gloxinia, primulas and polyanthus. All of them produce masses of flowers that will last for months.

a pretty spring flowerbox

In autumn pot up some miniature daffodils into a pretty container that has been filled with specially formulated bulb potting mix. Plant some alyssum or lobelia seedlings around the edges. Water the container once a week through the winter months, and in spring you will be rewarded with a colourful pot of sunny yellow daffodils framed by blue and white flowers.

a garden of flowers

Most plants produce flowers – it is an essential part of their reproductive cycle. The ones we most enjoy growing are those that are large and showy and create a colourful display. Flowering plants generally like lots of sun and they need quite good soil if they are to grow vigorously, and stay healthy. Plants that are grown in poor soil will always struggle, and this makes them more likely to be attacked by pests and diseases. The same applies with watering. If you forget to water your plants, their flowers will droop and look miserable.

flowering shrubs and perennials

Shrubs and perennials are useful plants because they are a permanent part of the garden, and they will keep flowering year after year if they are well cared for. Roses are shrubs, as are hydrangeas, azaleas and most kinds of daisy bushes. Generally shrubs do best when they are planted in well-prepared garden beds – not just in the lawn. Lawn will compete for moisture and nutrients, whereas shrubs planted in a garden bed can be mulched and this will help keep the weeds away from the base of the plants, and also help prevent the soil from drying out between watering. After flowering it's a good idea to prune back the shrubs – this usually just means cutting off the flower stems that have died. This keeps the plants compact, and also makes them look much tidier.

flowering bulbs

There are many flowering plants that grow from bulbs or corms, and these include daffodils and jonquils, tulips, dahlias, iris, lilies, snowdrops, gladiolus and hyacinths. These are marvellous plants for the garden because they die back during the winter, then burst into flower when the weather warms in spring. There are different bulbs for different climates, so choose the ones that are best suited to where you live. Most bulbous plants multiply under the ground and they can be dug up every few years, after the flowers and foliage have died back, and then divided to produce several clumps that can be replanted in different parts of the garden.

flowering annuals

Annuals are plants that only last for one season, and therefore you will need to plant fresh seeds or seedlings every year to get a new display of flowers. Usually planting is done in the spring, and depending on the variety of annual, the flowers will appear from summer right through until autumn. Popular flowering annuals include alyssum, cornflowers, poppies, marigolds, sunflowers, pansies, snapdragons, nasturtiums and stocks. Like all plants, annuals need to be looked after. Keep the weeds from smothering them by mulching around the plants once they have become established, and remember to water every few days during hot, dry weather to keep them growing strongly.

a self-sown flower garden

Annual plants produce seed heads when the flowers have faded and if left to ripen, these will scatter in the garden and produce new plants the following spring and summer. This is a great way to fill up the garden with colour, without having to buy seedlings from the nursery. Self-seeding annuals include forget-me-nots, California poppies, Oriental poppies, aquilegias, hellebores and paper daisies.

a flower picking garden Just as vegetables and herbs are usually grown in separate garden beds, you can also create a garden bed that is specifically for growing 'cut' flowers just for bringing indoors and arranging in a vase. Choose a sunny place and get the garden ready, just as you would for growing vegetables. Sow seeds of your favourite flowers, or buy mixed seed packets that contain a variety of colourful flowering annuals.

Lots of flowering plants have a wonderful fragrance and some gardeners select their plants for this reason alone. Many old-fashioned varieties of rose are highly perfumed, but also consider frangipani, stocks, freesias, lilies and sweet peas.

planting flowers

Flowering plants need water and fertiliser to grow well.
Pull out weeds that may crowd the plants as they grow, and mulch
around the base to help keep the soil from drying out too quickly.

step two Dig a hole for each seedling, following the directions about the distance apart they need to be planted. This should be written on the label of the punnet.

step one Prepare the soil by digging out any weeds and adding some homemade compost or well rotted cow manure to provide nutrients that will help the flowers to grow.

step three Carefully separate the seedlings, making sure that each small plant has a section of healthy roots. It's important to get the seedlings into the ground immediately.

You can also grow flowers from seed that can be sown directly in the ground. Tiny seeds, like red poppies, only need to be scattered on the soil and watered. However larger seeds need to be covered by the soil to germinate.

step four Place each seedling into the prepared hole and push the soil back around the roots. Press down lightly to keep the seedlings firmly in place.

step five Water the seedlings in well. This helps the plants to adjust and encourages the growth of vigorous new roots.

step six Cut the flowers if you want to make pretty posies for the house. If you like to leave the flowers growing in the garden, cut all the dead flowers off to encourage new flowers to bloom.

african violets

African violets are delightful perennials that are generally grown indoors, producing blue, purple, mauve, pinkish or white flowers for many months of the year. They are easy-care plants providing you know just a few tricks about their growing requirements.

about African violets

They are called African violets because the plants originally grew wild in Tanzania and other tropical regions of Africa. The flowers look a little bit like true violets, but in fact they are not related. The foliage is very attractive, usually rounded leaves with a velvety texture. When the flowers appear they are on slender stems in large clusters, making a very colourful display. Some of the flowers are edged in white, which is particularly pretty.

growing African violets

These houseplants like a bright, light position but they do not enjoy direct sunlight on their leaves or flowers. They will have been potted into a soil mix in a specialist nursery, and this should be enough to keep them growing well for a year or so. After that they should be potted again, into a mix that has been designed just for African violets. Take care not to over-water, as this is the most common cause of failure. Allow the soil to dry out between watering, and use water that is room temperature (not very cold water straight from the tap). Test the soil with your fingertip – if it is still damp the plant does not need to be watered. You can also buy special African violet fertiliser, and this is probably the safest option, as it will contain exactly the right balance of nutrients. The plants should only require feeding once or twice a year – in spring and again in mid summer.

did you know?

There is a very rare yellow-flowering African violet – all the others are in the white to pink, blue and purple colour range.

daisies

There are many plants that go by the common name 'daisy' and they include shrubs and perennials that have flat, open faces and often a yellow centre. These are all members of the same very large plant family, and they are loved because they are easy to grow and produce such cheerful blooms.

about daisies

Plants with characteristic daisy flowers include lovely little *Bellis perennis* (English daisies) which can be grown in the lawn and chrysanthemums, which come in many different colours, shapes and sizes. Even the tough and easy to grow *Erigeron* (seaside daisy) has those typical little flowers in various shades of pink and white. Every country in the world has its own group of plants with daisy flowers, which is why these plants are easy to grow in so many different climates.

growing daisies

Little English daisies can be planted along the edge of a garden bed, or the seed can be scattered in the lawn to produce a lovely carpet of flowers in late spring. Most daisies like lots of sun, which encourages them to produce masses of flowers. Daisies can be planted in spring and summer and even in autumn if you live in a warm climate. In the wild they are found growing in open, dry places, which means they need soil that has good drainage. So if you have clay soil make sure to dig in lots of organic matter prior to planting. The best favour you can do your daisy bushes is to keep picking those lovely flowers. It helps to keep the plant compact and also stimulates the growth of even more blooms.

did you know?

Members of the daisy family produce a lot of sweet nectar, which makes them valuable plants for beekeepers who place their hives in fields of wild daisies to produce the most delicious honey.

lavender

One of the world's most popular flowering shrubs, lavender has been cultivated for centuries as one of the main fragrant plants used for making perfumes and cosmetics. In the home garden there are dozens of different lavender varieties to choose from, with flowers than range from white through mauve and pink to deepest purple.

about lavender

Lavender plants are thought to have originated in Asia, but very quickly spread through southern Europe and the Mediterranean, where they can still be seen growing wild. Lavender can also be seen planted in huge fields in southern France, where the flowers are harvested for their essential oils used in the perfume industry. Most lavenders have soft grey green foliage and bright flower spikes that are highly fragrant.

growing lavender

Lavender is one of the easiest plants to grow because it prefers soil that isn't too rich and can get by without frequent watering, even during very hot summers. Lavender flowers in late spring and summer and can be planted at any time of year except mid winter. In the wild lavender grows in dry, rocky soil and this gives us a clue about the best growing conditions. If you have clay soil you may be best growing lavender in terracotta pots – these are porous and allow the potting soil to remain aerated. Lavender plants can become very straggly unless they are pruned back hard after flowering. So pick the blooms as often as you like, and then tidy up the plant when the last flowers have finished. You will be rewarded with even more flowers the following season.

did you know?

Although the entire lavender plant is fragrant, the essential oils are only contained in the tips of the buds, which is why they have such a concentrated aroma. Lavenders are also used by beekeepers to produce fragrant lavender honey.

the flower garden

snapdragons

These cute plants have unusual shaped flowers that appear to resemble the head of a dragon, with a mouth that can snap open and closed when you gently squeeze the sides of each bloom. Hence the common name snapdragon. They are available as seeds and seedlings in a bright range of flower colours, from white through shades of yellow, gold, orange, pink and crimson.

about snapdragons

These cheerful plants have always been popular with children and are a great addition to any flower gardens. They are in fact biennials, which means they grow and continue to flower for two years, however most people treat them as annuals and plant fresh seed or seedlings once a year. There are tall growing and also dwarf varieties and they are most dramatic when planted in a large clump to get a massed-flowering display.

growing snapdragons

You can plant seed or seedlings of snapdragons in autumn and they will just grow slowly during winter and then burst into full growth and flower in early spring. You can also plant seedlings in springtime, and this means you will have flowers right through until autumn. They like lots of sun and well-drained soil and the flowers should be clipped off when they start to die back because this will keep the plants compact and encourage the growth of more flowers.

did you know?

Snapdragons are very tough little plants, and can even survive in cold climates where there is frost in winter.

sunflowers

The happy golden faces of sunflowers are one of the highlights of the summer garden, and there are now so many varieties to choose from including dwarf forms and those with bronze, burgundy and terracotta as well as multi-coloured blooms tipped with yellow and pink.

about sunflowers

Sunflowers are in the same family as daisies, and they are loved because their flowers are so enormous and colourful. They are called sunflowers because the flowers literally turn their faces towards the sun and when you see them growing in a field every single bloom is facing the same direction. Sunflowers like warm weather and should be planted in the spring. If you live in a warm climate you can plant more seeds in summer, to flower during autumn.

growing sunflowers

Sunflowers must have a sunny, open position and soil that is quite rich with organic matter, but also has good drainage. So dig the garden bed well, and add lots of compost and well rotted manures before planting. The tall varieties are best grown in a clump, which helps prevent them from being knocked over on windy days. Or you can use stakes to support them, especially as the flowers appear – they can be so huge that the whole plant will topple over!

step one Scatter sunflower seeds onto the soil, then cover with 2cm (¾ inch) potting mix or garden soil. Water in well and make sure the pot or garden bed is in a sunny position.
step two When the seedlings appear, thin them out if they are too close together. Gently lift them out of the soil, roots intact, and transplant into another pot or garden bed.
step three When the seedlings are 10cm (4 inches) tall, tie them to stakes to prevent them blowing over in the wind. Keep them well watered and make sure weeds are not growing around the base of the plants.

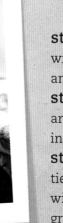

pressing flowers

Pressing flowers is a fun way to preserve memories using the flowers from your garden or from a bouquet. Use your pressed flowers in a variety of crafts to make beautiful and sentimental displays.

using a microwave Microfleur kits are available online. Gather flowers in the morning or evening so they are not wilted by the sun. As soon as possible lay out the flowers on a piece of cotton fabric and, following kit instructions, microwave the flowers until they are stiff and feel dry. Layer the dried flowers in between sheets of greaseproof paper in an airtight container until you're ready to use them.

using a book Use a thick, heavy book and open it up to the middle. Place a piece of tissue paper across both pages. Pick flowers in the early morning or evening so they are dry then place them on one side of the tissue. Thick flowers can be trimmed or divided into sections. The best flowers for pressing are those with open, flat 'faces': most daisies are perfect, as well as pansies, old-fashioned roses and small gerberas. You could also use other interesting plants such as ivy, herbs or weeds.

picture frame Position dried flowers in a creative arrangement on a piece of paper. Once you're happy with the design, use a paintbrush to coat PVA glue to the underside of each flower then press gently onto the paper. Allow your flower picture dry. When it has completely dried, fit the picture into a frame.

book covering Cover a school book or diary with plain coloured paper. Arrange a variety of pressed leaves into the shape of a monster. Cut out arms and legs from cardboard then glue into position. Glue on buttons for eyes. Cover the book with clear plastic wrapping to protect the design from coming off.

bookmarks Cut cardboard into a bookmark and punch a hole in the top. Position pressed flowers into a design. Use a paintbrush to coat PVA glue to the underside of each flower then press gently onto the cardboard. Allow to dry completely then thread ribbon through the hole and tie in place.

gift cards Position pressed flowers on a blank card with coloured paper, ribbons, beads (anything you like) into your favourite design. Use a paintbrush to coat PVA glue to the underside of each item, then press gently onto the card.

water gardens

When you have water in the garden it will become a haven for wildlife, including frogs who will come naturally into the garden, attracted to this welcoming environment.

step one Use a shallow container that is large enough to hold two or three small water plants and some rocks for encouraging frogs. Position it in a semi-shaded part of the garden.

step two Place some flat rocks in the centre of your container so that when the frogs eventually decide to make it home, they can easily get out of the water when they need to.

step three Half fill the container with water. Rain water from a tank is best for frogs as it contains no chlorine or other chemicals. Frogs have very sensitive skin.

Suitable aquatic plants are dwarf water lilies, dwarf sagittaria, dwarf water lobelia, typha minima (dwarf reed). These may only be available from water garden specialists.

step four Choose plants in pots from the water garden section of your local nursery and cover the soil surface with gravel or river stones to prevent the soil from floating away.

step five Position the water plants in the container and top up the water level so the pond is full. You may need to add more water every week if the weather is hot and dry.

step six Frogs will be attracted to the pond and should appear, even in city gardens, after several months. Don't introduce frogs from other regions as they do not enjoy being moved from their original home.

water gardens

A small water garden can be used for growing miniature aquatic plants. Choose a sheltered place with dappled shade and place a seat nearby so you can sit and enjoy the restful atmosphere.

making a terrarium

Terrariums work because they are an enclosed environment where the balanced humidity and temperature keep the plants healthy and happy.

step one Choose a glass container with a lid. You can find special terrarium containers, or simply use a glass fish tank that has a cover to prevent the environment from drying out.

step two Add a layer of gravel in the base of the container. This will provide drainage so that the plants are not sitting permanently in waterlogged soil.

step three Cover the gravel with a thin layer of sphagnum moss to stop the soil from dropping down to the bottom of the container. Then cover with a good, thick layer of rich potting soil.

step four Carefully plant a variety of small growing ferns and mosses. The aim is to create a garden in miniature so look for plants with a variety of different foliage colours and textures.

step five Introduce a little whimsy with decorative mushrooms or any other small ornament that takes your fancy. It is fun to create an indoor garden that is magical and mysterious.

step six Water the garden once a week, or more often if it appears to dry out. It should be positioned in a light, bright place but not in direct sunlight.

making a terrarium

A terrarium is like a miniature garden that you can enjoy inside. It's such fun to watch these small plants thrive in their home under glass.

my garden year

Keep a record of your activities in the garden by writing down when seeds have been planted, when seedlings are ready to go out into the vegetable patch and when you harvested.

january

What flowers I planted

....

....

What vegetables I planted

....

....

....

What I harvested

....

....

....

What problems I solved

....

....

....

....

february

What flowers I planted

....

....

What vegetables I planted

....

....

....

What I harvested

....

....

....

What problems I solved

....

....

....

Stick your
favourite pressed
flower here

march

What flowers I planted
....
....

What vegetables I planted
....
....

What I harvested
....
....

What problems I solved
....
....
....

Add your
photo here

april

What flowers I planted
....
....

What vegetables I planted
....
....

What I harvested
....
....

What problems I solved
....
....
....

may

What flowers I planted

....

....

What vegetables I planted

....

....

What I harvested

....

....

....

What problems I solved

....

....

....

....

Stick your
favourite pressed
flower here

june

What flowers I planted

....

....

What vegetables I planted

....

....

What I harvested

....

....

What problems I solved

....

....

....

july

What flowers I planted

....

....

What vegetables I planted

....

....

What I harvested

....

....

What problems I solved

....

....

....

....

august

What flowers I planted

....

....

What vegetables I planted

....

....

What I harvested

....

....

What problems I solved

....

....

....

september

What flowers I planted

....

....

What vegetables I planted

....

....

....

What I harvested

....

....

What problems I solved

....

....

....

....

october

What flowers I planted

....

....

What vegetables I planted

....

....

....

What I harvested

....

....

What problems I solved

....

....

....

Stick your
favourite pressed
flower here

november

What flowers I planted

....
....

What vegetables I planted

....
....

What I harvested

....
....

What problems I solved

....
....
....

december

What flowers I planted

....
....

What vegetables I planted

....
....

What I harvested

....
....

What problems I solved

....
....
....

what went wrong?

Sometimes, no matter how careful we are, the plants in our garden are damaged by pests or diseases and this can be very disappointing. Here are some common garden problems with tips on how to prevent them, or how to help your plants get healthy and happy again.

Why have my tomatoes turned white with brown patches on them?
During the hot summer the tomato fruits can be scalded by too much sunlight. It helps if you leave quite a lot of foliage on the plants to shade the tomatoes, or you could tie an umbrella to the top of the tomato stake to protect them from the harsh midday sun.

My tomato plants have a white powdery-looking mildew all over the leaves. Will this ruin the fruits?
Too much moisture on the foliage causes the mildew and while it won't kill the tomatoes, it will make the plants weak. Only water the plants at ground level with a good slow trickle from the hose. Always avoid letting the leaves get wet. Pull off any foliage that looks unhealthy and put it in the rubbish bin to prevent the mildew from spreading.

My flower seedlings fell over during the night and it looks like someone cut them with scissors at ground level. What has happened?
A nasty little caterpillar called a cutworm has chewed through your plants just where the stem comes out of the ground. When you plant some new seedlings place a old cardboard toilet roll around each plant and these pests can't do any more damage. When the plant gets bigger and stronger it will be safe from attack and you can remove the protective cardboard.

The buds of my roses are all covered with tiny white crawling insects that stop them from opening into flowers. Should I spray them with something?
Those little sap-sucking pests are called aphids and precious ladybugs just love to eat them, which is why you should never use a chemical spray. It will also kill the ladybugs. Instead you can squish them with your fingers (wearing gloves) while making sure not to mangle the flower buds, or you can spray them away with the hose on a fast jet setting. You may need to look again a few days later to make sure they haven't come back.

What is eating my cabbages – the leaves are covered with hundreds of little holes?
There is a white moth that flies around the garden and lays eggs on the leaves of cabbage plants. The eggs hatch out into tiny white caterpillars that make themselves very fat eating your cabbages. Once a week sprinkle a fine white layer of Derris Dust over the cabbage leaves – it's not a dangerous poison but it will stop the moth from laying eggs. Make sure you wash the cabbage leaves before eating them.

Every night snails come out from their hiding places and attack everything in my vegetable garden. I don't like squashing them, so what should I do?

Only water the garden in the early morning. Snails and slugs need moisture to slither around, and if the ground has become dry during the day it will be harder for them move around. Also leave a saucer of beer near the plants they love to eat – they will be attracted to the sugar and yeast and drown in the saucer. I have a couple ducks living in the garden and they eat all the snails and slugs. They are very happy, and so am I.

My carrots had lots of bushy green tops but when I pulled them up the carrot part was only tiny. What went wrong?

Carrots don't like soil that is too rich in nitrogen so avoid using poultry manure when preparing the garden for planting. The nitrogen causes the foliage to grow like crazy, but not the root (carrot) of the plant. Use blood and bone when digging the soil for planting carrots.

My lettuce plants sent up tall shoots with flowers on the top before we had time to harvest them. How can I prevent this from happening?

Only plant a few lettuce seedlings at once, as they will quickly develop flowering stems if left in the ground for too long, especially during hot summer weather. Plant six seedlings every three or four weeks, and that will give you a steady supply of lovely crisp lettuce for your salads.

We have possums in our garden and they come down at night and eat all the flower buds. How can we protect the plants?

Try leaving out some alternative food for the possums, well away from your flowering plants. They like fruit such as apples and pears, and this should keep them from attacking the garden. Another idea is to sprinkle some blood and bone around the plants because it has a strong smell, which the possums do not like.

My pot plants are swarming with thousands of little black ants, and the plants don't look very happy. Are the ants attacking the plants?

No, the ants are nesting in the potting soil because it's very dry, and this is also why the plants are looking so unhealthy. Soak the pot in a bucket of water for an hour, then let the water drain away. Repot the plant using some fresh potting mix. Make sure that you water the plants regularly, and the ants won't come back again and the plants will be smiling. Always wear gloves when using potting mix and they will also protect you from being nipped by all those ants.

what went wrong?

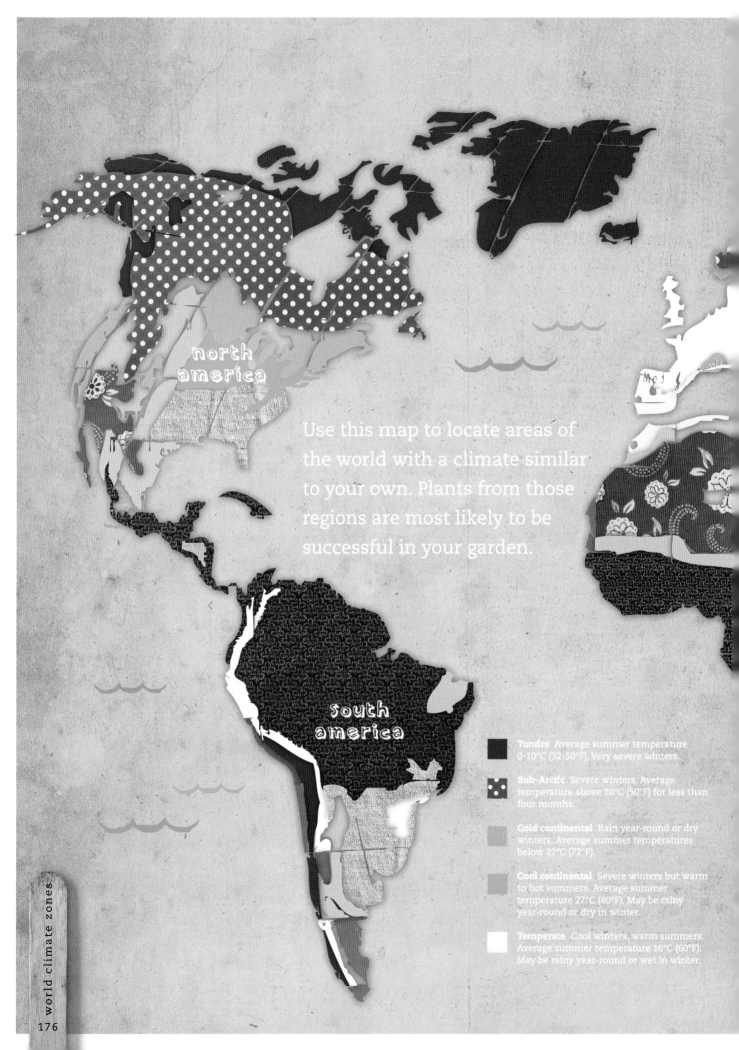

Use this map to locate areas of the world with a climate similar to your own. Plants from those regions are most likely to be successful in your garden.

north america

south america

Tundra Average summer temperature 0-10°C (32-50°F). Very severe winters.

Sub-Arctic Severe winters. Average temperature above 10°C (50°F) for less than four months.

Cold continental Rain year-round or dry winters. Average summer temperatures below 22°C (72°F).

Cool continental Severe winters but warm to hot summers. Average summer temperature 27°C (80°F). May be rainy year-round or dry in winter.

Temperate Cool winters, warm summers. Average summer temperature 16°C (60°F). May be rainy year-round or wet in winter.

world climate zones

europe

asia

rica

australia

Subtropical Cool to mild winters, warm to hot summers. Average summer temperature 27°C (80°F). May be rainy year-round or dry in winter.

Mediterranean Cool to mild winters, warm to hot summers. Average summer temperature 27°C (80°F). Summers dry.

Semi-arid plains Seasonal or evenly spread low rainfall. Average summer temperature 32°C (90°F). Cold or mild winters.

Desert Very low rainfall. Average summer temperature 38°C (100°F). Winters may be cold or mild.

Tropical Year-round warmth. High humidity, high rainfall, heaviest in summer; winters may be dry or less wet. Average summer temperature 27°C (80°F).

glossary
of gardening terms

annual
A plant that completes its life cycle within one year.

beneficial insects
Insects that are good for the garden because they control the insects that cause damage.

biennial
A plant that lives for 2 years, and may flower during both seasons.

bulbs
Plants that grow from swollen underground stems that store nutrients to feed the plant and make it grow eg daffodils.

clay soil
Soil with a high clay content which creates poor water drainage.

companion plants
Plants that should be grown side by side because they are good for each other.

compost
A heap of decomposed vegetable matter that is used as a soil builder.

dividing
A way of producing new plants by digging up the roots and separating them into two or more clumps for replanting. This really only works for bulbs and perennials.

dolomite lime
A soil additive that changes the pH level of the soil, making it more alkaline.

drainage
The ability of water to pass through the soil and not gather around plant roots.

fertiliser
A range of products used to feed plants and maintain healthy growth.

germination
When a seed produces a shoot that will eventually grow into a plant.

liquid fertiliser
A plant food that is mixed with water and applied around the base of a plant.

mulch
A layer of organic material used to prevent weeds from growing and also to prevent the soil from drying out too quickly.

organic matter
Manures and composts that are used to make the soil healthy and better for growing plants.

perennial
A plant that lives for a number of years. Some perennials die back in the autumn and grow back again in spring. Other perennials have permanent above ground foliage, similar to a shrub.

pollination
When male and female flowers are crossed to produce seed that will grow into a new plant.

potting mix
A light soil mix used for growing plants in containers. As soon as you open a bag of potting mix, walk away immediately and allow the spores to disperse into the air before you handle it.

pruning
Cutting back plants to encourage a more tidy, compact shape and more flowers.

sandy soil
Soil that has very free drainage and loses water quickly after watering or rainfall.

seedling
A small plant that has been grown under cover to a height of about 10-12cm (4-5 inches) and is ready for transplanting into the garden.

shrub
A woody plant that has stems and branches that grow from the base. They don't have a main trunk (like a tree).

thinning out
Removing unwanted plants that have germinated when seeds have been planted too close together.

watering in
When you water seeds or seedlings straight after they've been planted. Use a watering can as the spray of the hose can dislodge tiny seeds or plants.

glossary
of cooking terms

balsamic vinegar
Originally from Modena, Italy, there are now many on the market ranging in pungency and quality depending on how, and for how long, they have been aged. Quality can be determined up to a point by price; use the most expensive sparingly.

bicarbonate of soda
A raising agent also known as baking soda.

breadcrumbs, packaged
Prepared fine-textured but crunchy white breadcrumbs; good for coating foods that are to be fried.

burghul
Also called bulghur wheat; hulled steamed wheat kernels that, once dried, are crushed into various sized grains. Used in Middle Eastern dishes such as felafel and tabbouleh. Is not the same as cracked wheat.

cheese, parmesan
Also called parmigiano; a hard, grainy cow's-milk cheese originating in the Parma region of Italy. The curd is salted in brine for a month, then aged for up to 2 years.

cheese, ricotta
A soft, sweet, moist, white cow's-milk cheese with a low fat content and a slightly grainy texture. Its name roughly translates as "cooked again" and refers to ricotta's manufacture from whey that is itself a by-product of other cheese making.

chickpeas (garbanzo beans)
An irregularly round, sandy-coloured legume. Available canned or dried (reconstitute for several hours in cold water before use).

cornflour (cornstarch)
Made from corn or wheat; used as a thickening agent.

cream, pouring
Also called pure cream; it has no additives, and contains a minimum fat content of 35%.

cumin
Also called zeera or comino; resembling caraway in size, is the dried seed of a parsley-related plant. Has a spicy, curry-like flavour; is available dried as seeds or ground.

flour, plain (all-purpose)
Unbleached wheat flour.

flour, self-raising
All-purpose flour with added baking powder and salt; make at home in the proportion of 1 cup flour to 2 teaspoons baking powder. Also called self-rising flour.

green onions (scallions)
Also called (incorrectly) shallots; an immature onion picked before the bulb has formed, having a long, bright-green edible stalk.

oil, vegetable
Any of a number of oils sourced from plant rather than animal fats.

pine nuts
Also called pignoli; not a nut but a small, cream-coloured kernel from pine cones. They are best roasted before use to bring out the flavour.

pomegranate
Darkred, leathery-skinned fresh fruit about the size of an orange filled with hundreds of seeds, each wrapped in an edible lucent-crimson pulp having a unique tangy sweet-sour flavour.

prosciutto
An unsmoked Italian ham; salted, air-cured and aged, it is usually eaten uncooked.

sugar, caster (superfine)
Also called finely granulated table sugar.

sugar, icing (confectioners')
Also called powdered sugar; pulverised granulated sugar crushed together with a small amount of cornflour.

tahini
Sesame seed paste available from Middle Eastern food stores.

wholegrain mustard
Also called seeded; french-style coarse-grain mustard made from crushed mustard seeds and dijon mustard.

conversion chart

measures

One Australian metric measuring cup holds approximately 250ml; one Australian metric tablespoon holds 20ml; one Australian metric teaspoon holds 5ml.

The difference between one country's measuring cups and another's is within a two- or three-teaspoon variance, and will not affect your cooking results. North America, New Zealand and the United Kingdom use a 15ml tablespoon.

All cup and spoon measurements are level. The most accurate way of measuring dry ingredients is to weigh them. When measuring liquids, use a clear glass or plastic jug with metric markings.

We use large eggs with an average weight of 60g.

dry measures

METRIC	IMPERIAL
15g	½oz
30g	1oz
60g	2oz
90g	3oz
125g	4oz (¼lb)
155g	5oz
185g	6oz
220g	7oz
250g	8oz (½lb)
280g	9oz
315g	10oz
345g	11oz
375g	12oz (¾lb)
410g	13oz
440g	14oz
470g	15oz
500g	16oz (1lb)
750g	24oz (1½lb)
1kg	32oz (2lb)

liquid measures

METRIC	IMPERIAL
30ml	1 fluid oz
60ml	2 fluid oz
100ml	3 fluid oz
125ml	4 fluid oz
150ml	5 fluid oz (¼ pint)
190ml	6 fluid oz
250ml	8 fluid oz
300ml	10 fluid oz (½ pint)
500ml	16 fluid oz
600ml	20 fluid oz (1 pint)
1000ml (1 litre)	1¾ pints

length measures

METRIC	IMPERIAL
3mm	⅛in
6mm	¼in
1cm	½in
2cm	¾in
2.5cm	1in
5cm	2in
6cm	2½in
8cm	3in
10cm	4in
13cm	5¼in
15cm	6in
18cm	7¼in
20cm	8in
23cm	9¼in
25cm	10in
28cm	11¼in
30cm	12in (1ft)

oven temperatures

These oven temperatures in this book are for conventional ovens; if you have a fan-forced oven, decrease the temperature by 10-20 degrees.

	°C (CELSIUS)	°F (FAHRENHEIT)
Very slow	120	250
Slow	150	300
Moderately slow	160	325
Moderate	180	350
Moderately hot	200	400
Hot	220	425
Very hot	240	475

index

general index

recipe index

Published in 2011 by ACP Books, Sydney
ACP Books are published by ACP Magazines,
a division of Nine Entertainment Co.

Acp Books

General manager Christine Whiston
Editor-in-chief Susan Tomnay
Creative director Hieu Chi Nguyen
Art director & designer Hannah Blackmore
Senior editor Stephanie Kistner
Food director Pamela Clark
Author Mary Moody
Sales & rights director Brian Cearnes
Marketing manager Bridget Cody
Senior business analyst Rebecca Varela
Operations manager David Scotto
Production manager Victoria Jefferys

Printed by Toppan Printing Co., China.
Australia Distributed by Network Services
Phone +61 2 9282 8777 Fax +61 2 9264 3278
networkweb@networkservicescompany.com.au
New Zealand Distributed by Southern Publishers Group,
Phone +64 9 360 0692 Fax +64 9 360 0695 hub@spg.co.nz
South Africa Distributed by PSD Promotions,
Phone +27 11 392 6065/6/7 Fax +27 11 392 6079/80
orders@psdprom.co.za

Photographer **Maree Homer**
Stylist **Louise Bickle**
Craft stylist **Olivia Blackmore**
Cover photochef **Jordanna Levin**

Published by ACP Books,
a division of ACP Magazines Ltd.
54 Park St, Sydney NSW Australia 2000
GPO Box 4088, Sydney, NSW 2001
Phone +61 2 9282 8618
Fax +61 2 9126 3702
acpbooks@acpmagazines.com.au
www.acpbooks.com.au

*The publishers would like to thank the following for the gardens
used in photography:* Booth/McClintock family, Crown Street
Public School, Gaffney/Hausler family, Homer family, James
Street Community Garden, George Kambesis, Lewis/Teal
family, Le Masurier family, Mahony family, Middleton/
Matthews family, Prodes family, Prodes/Bickle family,
Raftos/Norman family.

*The publishers would also like to thank the following for props
used in photography:* Flower Power www.flowerpower.com.au;
Garden Life www.gardenlife.com.au; Ici et La www.icietla.
com.au; Tumbleweed www.tumbleweed.com.au; No Chintz
Textiles and Soft Furnishings www.nochintz.com

To order books phone 136 116 (within Australia),
or order online at www.acpbooks.com.au
Send recipe enquiries to:
recipeenquiries@acpmagazines.com.au

A catalogue record for this book is available
from the National Library of Australia.
ISBN: 978-1-74245-130-5 (pbk.)
© ACP Magazines Ltd 2011
ABN 18 053 273 546